Jolly Jaunts
with
The Parson and The Publican

Worcestershire, Herefordshire
& The Wye Valley

Revd Ian Charlesworth and Richard Stockton Esq.

Jolly Jaunts is published by Black Pear Media, Evesham

ISBN 978-0-9574567-0-9

First published 2012

BLACK (PEAR) MEDIA
Connecting the Heart of England

Contents

AUTUMN

WINTER

Revd Ian Charlesworth

From an early age The Parson has loved to lift the latch and discover the wonder contained within the parish churches of the land. As Rector of five churches in the Wye Valley he knows full well how much care and attention such places require but also the pleasure and solace they can bring. The story of generations of worshippers contained therein is compelling and should be celebrated, as should the countless hours put in by volunteers to keep such places open. This is thirsty work and so a little something to lay the dust of ages is always welcome.

Richard Stockton Esq.

The Publican is a simple soul whose tastes reflect his pleasures. Having for many years lived the dream as Innkeeper of a fine local hostelry catering for the lover of country sports, good food and a well kept pint he now divides his time between the garden, the easel and the pursuit of the perfect pint of Pippin juice. This last lures him across the threshold of many a watering hole. The enthusiasm and passion for good, local, seasonal food and drink that he often finds therein gives him hope that the tide of brushed stainless steel and stripped, pale wood will not overwhelm the pubs of this land.

Acknowledgements

First and foremost, thanks and praise go to our Senior Managements. They remind us that we are due to be out and about, make sure we are reasonably and tidily turned out and prepared for all weathers. We are indebted to assorted offspring, family and friends who have endured the ramblings, embarrassments and other risks associated with being seen out with two such persistent potterers.

Great gratitude is owed to Joanne Goodwin of Herefordshire & Wye Valley Life who responded so enthusiastically to our first contact and has allowed us to appear in numerous publications despite our inability to recognise a deadline. Similarly, Jane Sullivan, as editor of Worcestershire Life, put us in print for the first time, gave us another county to play in and has taken on the task of shaping this little offering.

Finally, we would like to pay tribute to all the wonderful people who have made our Jaunts so Jolly: the innkeepers, landlords and ladies, the cooks, chefs and waiting staff, the purveyors of coffee and cake, the churchwardens, volunteers and enthusiasts who keep churches open and welcoming, and the local businesses, farmers and food producers that make these counties such great places to live and visit. Long may they flourish.

Burford

BEWDLEY

TENBURY
WELLS

Cotheridge
& Knightwick

Malvern

UPTON
UPON
SEVERN

Inkberrow

WYRE FOREST

BROMSGROVE

FECKENHAM

WORCESTER CITY

EVESHAM

Bretforton

Broadway

NORTIMER

Hay-on-Wye

KINGTON

GOLDEN
VALLEY

Craswall

Abbeydore

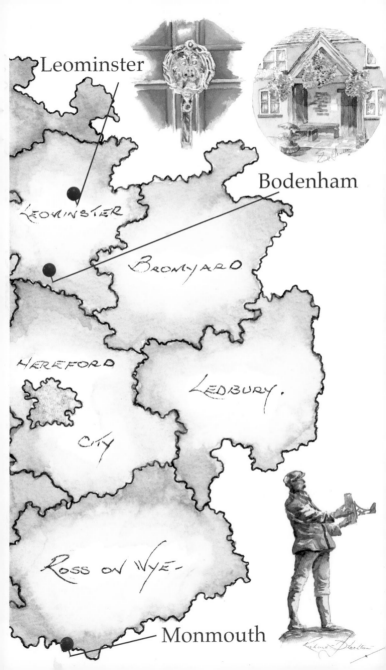

Leominster

Bodenham

LEOMINSTER

BROMYARD

HEREFORD

LEDBURY.

CITY

ROSS ON WYE.

Monmouth

Jolly Jaunts
in the Spring

THE PARSON'S IDLE THOUGHTS

In the beginning

A SIMPLE enough request one would have thought; what the modern manager would call a 'task and finish' operation. After many years behind the bar the Publican had retired and taken to pottering with an alacrity that surprised us all. Of course, what we called pottering he saw as gainful employment but it meant that he was out and about in the fresh air and each evening, as well as a fresh anecdote to tell, he had an excuse for a glass of something to lay the dust.

All-in-all an admirable arrangement that ensured he was out from under the feet of Senior Management without tying him down too firmly. So, when a new sofa needed to be collected from the outskirts of Hereford he was clearly going to be available for the job. As his designated carer, where forays into the world were concerned, it was a natural assumption that I would accompany him. The fact that my vehicle, with the seats removed, was capable of carrying the aforementioned soft furnishing sealed the deal.

A cold day in early spring saw us, sofa located and loaded, on the 'other' side of Hereford just as it began to dawn that the lunching hour was drawing close. No doubt you know the moment well; the solidity of a good breakfast is a thing of the past, and elevenses but a distant memory. As the sun, influential in these matters even when obscured by cloud, rises to the meridian the juices start to flow and the mind finds it hard to concentrate on much else but the locating and consuming of the necessary calories. With any luck these will be warm and tasty and some of them will come wrapped up in a cool draught of malted barley, flavoured with hops and fermented to the peak of perfection. It is the old hunter-gatherer instinct I suspect.

The Old Licensed Victualler and I found ourselves so placed when it occurred to him that the 'other' side of Hereford was the Carey side of Hereford and there was to be found the Cottage of Content whose landlord had been a patron of The Griffin when a variety of beautiful 'nieces' needed a bed for the night.

It was but the work of a moment to point the radiator grill in the general direction and hope for the best. Our beast of burden did not disappoint and before the pangs of hunger overwhelmed us we were pulling up outside the hostelry ready for refreshment. Oh Calamity! The innkeeper had found love and was at that very moment taking his uxorious pleasures in a bridal suite elsewhere. 'Gone on Honeymoon' chalked upon a board hung carelessly upon the latch. Whilst the better part of our natures rejoiced in his good fortune our stomachs and increasingly dry throats thought it a pretty rum do as we dejectedly turned away from the Cottage of Content.

We re-embarked and I turned the car for the journey home when I saw a signpost indicating that the village of Hoarwithy was not too far distant. I had recently read of an eccentric Vicar of that parish who had inspired such terror in some of the more susceptible members of the community that even as they lay dying, decades after his departure, they feared an encounter not with their Maker but with their former Incumbent. He had also had built a rather remarkable church. Loath to waste the journey and seeing lunch as a lost cause I suggested that we pay a visit en route and, meeting with little resistance, turned right and pushed on along the banks of the Wye.

The wonders of the parish church of St Katherine's, Hoarwithy, we have recorded elsewhere. Suffice to say, it was not a wasted journey and a good time was had by all. However, years of blood thinning and a recent lack of calorific intake had made the OLV particularly

St Katherine's, Hoarwithy

vulnerable to the penetrating cold and so, as we descended the steps to the road, the necessity of finding a fireside by which to park him became evident.

Fortunately just across the way The Harp appeared to be open for business and so we crossed the road, tottered over the threshold and collapsed, pale from undernourishment, into a conveniently placed sofa by the wood burner. By the time the food arrived we were sufficiently revived to start to take note of our surroundings and the plates in front of us.

As we consumed the much-needed victuals the discussion ranged widely. How to make a good gravy was given due consideration as was the pretension of food-flavoured foam (something looking like grasshopper goo was sitting in an embarrassed puddle in the middle of the OLV's soup). We thought a little about slate floors, pale oak and brushed stainless steel as decorating themes in the country pub and reminisced about country pubs of our youth, smoke-filled though they might have been. Together with some thoughts on the church it was as erudite a conference as you could have hoped to have overheard.

Being fond of words and enjoying the challenge we thought to record our various thoughts for the delectation and delight of our nearest and dearest and, with the addition of a few delicate watercolours, Prayers and Pints, the Parson and the Publican on a pottering pilgrimage was born.

Gate to Cottage of
Content, Carey

INKBERROW

St Peter's and The Old Bull

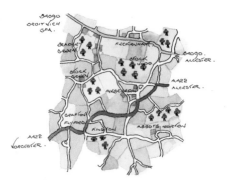

IT IS the perfect day to drive through the wonderful Worcestershire countryside. Every bank froths with blossom. The fresh green of the leaves shines in the warm sunshine. The winter is past; long, dark nights but a distant memory. However, it a dark deed, perpetrated on just such a frosty winter's night that draws us into the depths of the county on our latest jaunt. For despite the blossom, the bone-warming rays of sunshine and freshly-fringed hedgerows the Old Licensed Victualler is in something of a slough of despond. He sits beside me now, slumped into the worn leather upholstery, staring sightlessly at the passing scenery. Just to check on his vital signs I breathe the name

'Vanessa Whitburn'. It is as though a bolt of lightening has struck from a clear blue sky. Electrified, he sits up, thumps the dashboard, utters an imprecation too profane for your delicate ears, dear Reader, and reaches for his snuff. We are *en route* to Inkberrow to appease the shadow of the late Nigel Pargetter with a small libation in the Old Bull.

St Peter's Church

WHEN we arrive it is too early even for the OLV to partake and so we park under the newly-leafed horse chestnuts and wander through the lych gate to investigate the very attractive church of St Peter.

The approach to the church is everything an English country church should be. If the Old Bull is the archetype of Ambridge's watering-hole then this is what any child drawing a church would expect it to look like. Porch, tower, nave and chancel all beautifully in proportion, just the right number of pinnacles and a bit of crenelation around the top of the tower

The church itself is surprisingly large when we step into the nave. On our right a large chest is well provided with evidence of the many things this busy congregation gets up to. Amidst it all are two folders with a history of the church. One is kindly in large print so the OLV sits down to look at the pictures. He is soon on his feet again and chuckling in front of the chest the lid of which has been neatly sliced in two at some point. In common with many such chests it has three locks and required the Vicar and both churchwardens to be present with their keys to open it. Clearly once upon a time somebody lost theirs. I suggest that it was a churchwarden but rather suspect that it was the Vicar. I can well imagine the indulgent smile that hid an exasperated sigh as they sent for the village carpenter to wield his saw that they might get at the church plate and accounts.

This is a church of screens, and recent ones at that. Two beautifully carved examples form two areas of the north aisle. The westernmost one enclosing a space used as a vestry has angels very much of the 1970s, which are charming, and a depiction of King Charles I who left a map in the Rectory when he spent the night. One wonders if, when this was pointed out to him, he commented that he "would forget his head if it wasn't screwed on." Certainly he is shown with his head detached at the neck so maybe he was often forgetful. Surely there could be no other reason...

My little witticism is lost upon my companion who has turned to view the font. Square in shape and decorated with stylised flowers the damage around the lip, the guide tells us, was caused by the removal of iron staples that were part of the security system to protect the holy water within.

The tower, St Peter's

19

Sundial, St Peter's Church

We meander down the nave, noting the well-decorated children's area to one side behind another, more open, screen and then in the south transept we come upon the tomb of John Savage. A Jacobean worthy he is depicted in armour and once was surrounded by all ten of his children although some seem to have left him over time. His effigy is surmounted by a fine canopy supported by slender black columns. All in all it is a very restrained example of its type. There are three rather solemn-looking cherub faces presiding over the marble figure which has certainly suffered over time. He has every right, we discover, to compare himself to one of the ruins that Cromwell knocked about a bit since, within a few years of completion, that was indeed his fate.

With this monumental momento mori before us we are reminded of our sad task and so we make our way to the Old Bull to pay our respects.

The Old Bull

IT IS just as I imagined; half-timbered with two tiny windows peeping from the long, low-pitched, umber-tinted tile roof. Becalmed in a backwater adjacent to the village green, the inn is surrounded by tall trees where the constant cacophony tells of rooks going about their daily routine. Outside sit walkers with sturdy boots tucked under the picnic tables supping pints, chomping on cheese, brown baguettes and piquant pickles, their walking sticks at ease against the weather-worn benches. We lift the latch and enter the sacred sanctuary that is The Bull. I look around, eagerly anticipating the Grundys; Joe and Eddie hatching some scam with Snatch Foster or maybe Kenton sitting at the bar chatting up his new-found love. I long to believe that we are in Ambridge but my old chum the Parson insists it is Inkberrow. The old codger is a brutal realist. For all he tries to inspire us to be heavenly minded, to not covet the neighbour's eggs, or his pullet for that matter, he has earthy tendencies that frequently frustrate my flights of fancy. And talking of fancy is that Jolene behind the bar?

He has a pint of Shires while I, for a change, sample a mug of autumn sunshine from the orchard and we lift our glasses in silent salutation to the late, lamented, laird of Lower Loxley, butchered to make a Roman holiday my companion says. Byron, he mutters, and I look around for Mr Aldridge from my perch under the wide-screen television (Sid Perkes would put it on for important sporting events); he is not there. The scene before me is bucolic; shiny horse brasses adorn the many low beams, the bar is pleasantly cluttered and everywhere are photographs and memorabilia of the long-running radio series. The Parson surveys today's menu which is on a free-standing board on our table. It is honest and simple (a bit like us really) and what could be better? I am firmly of the belief that half a dozen well-cooked, home-made classics beat pompous platters any day.

Seldom, these days, is one able to find a pub that is not encompassed around with extensions for restaurants with their dark, oak-stained, wood tables dressed with white cloths and red paper napkins folded into glasses or

The Old Bull

the odd conservatory, complete with desiccated palm or pelargonium, festering on side of the original building. So it is a pleasure to see The Old Bull unencumbered. People have been sitting and supping between these walls for well over 250 years; the great Bard of Avon trod these very flagstones, reputably loitering here on his way to Worcester to collect his marriage licence. Thinking of bardic ancients I notice that the relic opposite is scratching the ecclesiastical pate which is always a sign of some anxiety to me. As usual he is indecisive so I order for him, which is just a question of leaning over and telling the barmaid, briefly interrupting her banter with the locals who are trying to find today's paper which is not in its usual place.

"Do you know," says I, still wistfully wishing myself in Ambridge. "I could have been at school with Sid Perkes. He was born in Moseley in Birmingham close to my first Alma Mata."

"Didn't he go to an approved school, having been done for breaking and entering, if memory serves me right?" enquires the Parson.

Crushed again by the ecclesiastical encyclopaedia I ignore this remark and continue. "Well he made a great success of this place and did a great job for the community; resurrecting the cricket club and the football team," I say. With a hint of Thou Shalt Not he replies with recollections of a steamy affair with a dancing teacher and the scandal of heavy breathing in the shower.

"Sshh!" I say, in warning, as the barmaid appears with our plates. "I dig into my ham and eggs but, oh dear, the chips, although golden brown, are not cooked. His 'pie' is clearly misnamed. A nodding glance towards the crisp perfection of a pastry topping is offered by the stale top of a vol-au-vent perched precariously on what is more of a sloppy and unappetising brown mess than the venison and bacon pie advertised. We are chomping in disappointed silence; when he leans over and says: "I think it must be Freda's day off." He does believe, really.

EZRA BAY IN THE POTTING SHED

Grasses

WE WERE sitting on the top step of the potting shed, Uncle Dick and I, with Monty the whippet between us, his head on his paws, tired out with chasing rabbits in the woods. It was evening and with the sun sinking to the west in a cloudless sky came that gentle calm heralding the end of a perfect working summer's day; with that magical time the seasonal scents seem somehow to be more intense. Not only the fruity aroma of the first bottle of last year's raspberry wine in the tin mugs, and the sweet scent of the two pots of night-scented stock placed either side of the steps but the unmistakeable smell of new-mown hay.

Common Blue butterflies on meadow grass

There are said to be not far short of four thousand species of grasses, from the dwarf grasses of the wild moors and mountains through the arable crops to the massive bamboos up to eighty feet tall found in the Tropics.

Of the more common resident British grasses there are well over a hundred; yet the only one

23

responsible for the classic smell of drying hay is Sweet Vernal Grass which contains a chemical called coumarin. Just a tiny amount of this rather non-descript plant gives the whole hay field this unique and well-loved perfume.

We love to hate the Common Couch Grass with its invasive and aggressive root system rather similar in appearance to the Perennial Rye Grass. I expect some of us gardeners may recognise Crested Dog's Tail, Timothy, Quaking, and the intriguingly named Yorkshire Fog. In July the bushy flower heads of this rather attractive grass are a delicate pinkish-green, deepening to mauve as they mature, and fading in the autumn to a pale grey. Its name is thought to derive from the Old Norse *fogg* meaning long, limp and damp. In North Country dialect 'fog' is any coarse winter grass that has grown after the hay has been mown and carted.

I watched the swallows feeding in the darkening sky and the swifts high above them, their long scythe-like wings gliding, interspersed with rapid wing beats as they gained height. It was once thought that they returned to their nests to roost after dark but it's now known that unless they are incubating they fly continually; feeding, sleeping and even mating on the wing. Their legs have almost disappeared through evolution but possess very strong hawk-like claws which are used to cling to vertical surfaces of tall buildings and to defend their territories with long and vicious combats with encroaching neighbours. They mate for life and have one clutch of two or three eggs, the fledged chicks flying after about five weeks.

Uncle Dick followed my gaze to the slowly disappearing birds; so high were they.

"Aye," he murmured. "A rare sight before May 1st and after September 1st and they fly in family groups and colonies all the way south of the Equator."

"Speaking of all gone," says Uncle Dick raising the bottle of depleted wine to the fast diminishing light. "We just as well finish 'er off."

"Now did I ever tell you the story of when I was a lad leading old Nell the black shire horse from over Lower Broadheath Farm carting the hay when 'er trod on me toes . . . ?"

CRASWALL

St Mary's and White Haywood Farm

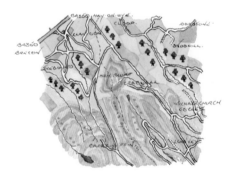

GENTLE reader you will be surprised to learn that we are a little nervous. We are in the delightful surroundings of Craswall Church and about to host the second of our outings for visitors to the Hay Festival; Event 890 to be precise, described in the Festival Programme thus: "Craswall Priory (ruined) and Parish Church lure the Parson and the Publican to their wonderful setting, nestling in the bosom of a hidden valley in the Black Mountains. A convivial supper in the Bull's Head to follow." All of it true – except the bit about the Priory ruins and the Bull's Head. The former was deemed too inaccessible even for our doughty bus driver and the latter too unreliable in its hours of opening to entrust to it the appetites of five and twenty hungry, thirsty seekers after enlightenment.

We had agreed that waiting by the kissing gate provided the best place for the bus to pull in when the grinding of gears reached our ears. The Old Licensed Victualler, perhaps ever hopeful that the gate might prompt the action, moved a touch closer and tugged at his cravat and I gave my shoes a surreptitious rub on the backs of the trouser legs. The bus rattled to a halt, the doors opened and a jolly looking bunch of chaps and chapesses disgorged with a view to an evening's entertainment.

Whilst the OLV was fully occupied helping the ladies down the step with a solicitous arm my attention was distracted by the Volvo that pulled up in a cloud of dust to the rear of the bus. A cheery face appeared from out the open window.

"Is this the walk?" I'm asked. "Well not really." I reply, "More an amble around a church and then off to supper. The Publican's knees are not up to anything more." Given the changes we had made I had a horrid feeling that a walker had strayed into our definitely non-energetic enterprise. "Oh" says he, "I must have followed the wrong bus. Can I stay?" The OLV and I are always of 'the-more-the-merrier' school of thought so I warmly encouraged him to do so and the would-be walker joins us.

St Mary's Church

L ONG and low, Craswall church is a simple building with a single roof line topped by a small wooden bell-cote. As far from grand as it is possible to be this is a church for farming folk who, for generations, have struggled to make a living off the upland pastures. Nothing fancy in their lives or their church, no unnecessary or expensive frills or furbelows yet it speaks of their determination to gather together for worship, education and fun.

It seems the church was built when the Priory was suppressed in the 1460s for being a foreign foundation and the suggestion is made in the guide book that the east window was relocated from there – evidence of both recycling and the ever thrifty hill farmer I suggest. Beautiful in its simplicity the interior of the church is furnished with free-standing, wooden pews whilst, around the walls, are numerous large, wooden pegs upon which one imagines the men would hang their hats, although it is hard to believe that there were ever as many people in the church as there are pegs.

At the east end the sanctuary is simple with altar, pulpit and modern stone font providing all that is necessary for Divine Service. Although very plain, traces of pre-Reformation decoration remain on the roof timbers above the altar where delicate flowers and foliage point to a more colourful past. At the west end a gallery, lit by a dormer window, provides extra seating up a narrow stair. Under the gallery a small door leads to a vestry.

In the 18th century the west end was separated by a wall from the rest of the church and this space used as a schoolroom entered through the substantial porch. Originally linked through an arched opening to the church this was blocked up to make a much smaller door. The OLV suggests that those at the back were fed up with the draughts.

It is fashionable these days to talk about making churches more

St Mary's Church

Jolly Jaunts

Window in the old school room,
St Mary's Church

available to the community. Craswall church has been doing just that probably since it was built. The schoolroom is just one example. When a new school was built in the 19th century this room was used by farmers to store their fleeces before they were taken down the hill. Fitted with a large shuttered window and a fireplace I dare say it has seen its fair share of meetings both sacred and secular.

Outside, we draw attention to the stone seat that runs around the south and west walls of the church, the court for hand tennis on the windowless north side, of which faint red lines can be traced in the plaster, and the cockpit in the north west corner of the churchyard, now overgrown with trees. It is not hard on an evening such as this to imagine the locals gathering to pass the time in gossip, flirting and games.

The company and the discussions are so engaging that it is just as well that Nick the Festival Steward is keeping his eye on the time.

With a gentle tap on the shoulder he reminds us that we must be moving on and since I notice that the OLV is getting a little carried away with the talk of games and flirting in the churchyard I join him in gently shepherding the flock to the awaiting charabanc.

White Haywood Farm

"IT WAS the smell," says Pauline. "That unforgettable stench of rotting flesh." She looks wistfully towards her husband, the only other witness to that terrible trauma just ten years ago.

We are sitting around the delightful little bar set in the corner of their tastefully restored, 400-year-old barn-cum-restaurant. We are at the end of an enjoyable evening my old chum the Parson and I; that magical, winding down time when, after service, if one is lucky one may get to know the hosts a little better over a privileged night cap.

"As fast as we could help the ewes with their lambs up this end," she continues. "They were being killed down that end," she points remotely to the other end of the barn.

"Luckily the girls were spared all that as they had to stay away when foot and mouth struck the farm," she looks at Rebecca and Abigail, their young daughters who had waitressed and looked after us so efficiently during the evening.

"The person I felt most sorry for though," she says in her typically unselfish manner, "was my dad, for although 'retired,' overnight his farming was finished; all the blood lines including his beloved Radnor sheep which he had selectively bred and nurtured over the years ended that day.

"It was over a week before they moved the carcasses," says Philip, husband, father, farmer, barman, waiter and no doubt pot-washer when the need arises.

Theirs is a not an uncommon story of hill farmers struggling to make a living in the face of all the odds. After every animal except the donkey was slaughtered these fourth generation farmers looked at ways to diversify. A talented self-taught cook Pauline started making savoury pies and quiches which she sold at the busy little Thursday market in Hay-on-Wye. Demand grew and, encouraged by her success, she started providing Sunday lunches in the farmhouse. The big decision was made four years ago when the old stone barn was converted into a restaurant. Philip went off to pull a pint or two at the nearby Bulls Head and is now a dab hand behind his little bar dispensing, amongst other beverages, some excellent pippin juice from Gwatkin's Moorhampton Park Farm in the next valley at Abbey Dore.

The secret to their success is simplicity. Meat, reared and given free range of the lush green pastures and natural spring water coming off the Black Hill, is cooked and served by the family. We were welcomed into the spacious stone barn and, of course, made our way to the bar where Philip and one of the girls were serving. An American lady wanting 'something local' was recommended the cider and the absent walker insisted on buying a bottle of wine; hoping someone would help him out with a glass or two.

"No problem there," says my old chum the Parson, hovering like a kestrel eyeing up a plump vole.

Seated, we are brought to order by the dulcet tones of Pauline who, used to calling the cattle and Philip to lunch over the distance of a couple of fields, knows how to captivate the audience. No complications of menus, she bawls, for tonight it's roast pork, beef or the vegetarian spinach and mushroom wellington. Pad and pencil? Not on your life; up go the hands and like sheep between hurdles we are counted.

The decibels rise so I can only see the ecclesiastical head nod at the offer of another glass of the tinto by the friendly absent walker. Slices of pink beef appear with crispy roast potatoes, Yorkshire puddings, like mother used to make, accompanied by steaming jugs of rich gravy and bowls of *al dente* vegetables. I sit with a family from Derbyshire whose growing son consumes the remains of every vacant

White Haywood Farm

vegetable bowl; what an appetite.

Puddings are classic with treacle and walnut tart coming high in the batting order and a really naughty thick creamy Pavlova smeared with Pauline's home-made lemon curd a generous chunk of which I notice is placed before the old codger.

We are much taken with White Haywood Farm restaurant and B & B and it is clear that we are not alone in this. Our departing guests one and all declare it to have a been a splendid evening. Senior Management informs me that an impending visit of family from distant shores is threatened. I have promised them Thursday's famous fish and chips; besides as we left Pauline offered to show me the bedrooms next time and, who knows, Philip may be shearing.

RECIPE

The Parson's chicken and leek pie

IT WILL not take a regular reader long to recognise that when it comes to food the OLV and I run true to type. If I am unable to make a decision when perusing the bill of fare then I can usually rely upon my companion to pick to my taste. Devotees, and such as keep note of such things, will often see a pie feature in that choice.

More often than not these are delicious; well if we are lucky they are. Variety is all, we have discovered. I have been presented with everything from the tenderest chunks of beef enrobed in a deeply-flavoured glossy gravy given depth by a local beer and slow cooking, all of it encased in a golden casket of pastry, shards of which glisten in the light as my knife presses through the laminated layers of loveliness; to a brown, dull slurry of little texture and no flavour topped with the a stale circle of pastry that once did duty as the top of a vol-au-vent at a funeral tea.

Rarely do we encounter a chicken pie and yet it is one of my favourites, simple to make and delicious. Served with roast potatoes and veg it is a crowd pleaser at the Rectory.

Chicken & Leek Pie
(serves 6-8)

INGREDIENTS

- 1 large chicken
- 1 small onion
- 2 carrots
- 5 rashers of smoked streaky bacon (it doesn't have to be streaky but it should be smoked)

Jolly Jaunts

- 3 medium leeks
- 2 oz butter
- A goodly amount (1½ well-heaped tablespoon) plain flour
- A proper dollop (2 tablespoons) crème fraiche (cream or milk will do just as well)
- Salt and freshly-ground black pepper
- 1 block shop-bought puff pastry

METHOD

1. Place the chicken in a large pan or casserole dish. Roughly chop the onion and carrot and place in the pan with the chicken. Cover with cold water and add some salt. Bring to the boil and then turn the heat down low and leave to simmer for two hours, or place in the oven at 160°C for the same length of time. This could be done the night before you want to eat the pie.
2. Once the chicken is cooked remove from the pan, saving the stock, to a board and strip the meat off the breast and legs. This is easier if you let it cool for a bit first. As you do so break the meat into reasonable-sized pieces and place in a large pie dish.
3. Chop the leeks and bacon. Melt the butter in a medium pan and then stir in the leeks and bacon. Cover and cook until soft, about five minutes, and then stir in the flour. Gradually add enough of the reserved stock, stirring well as you go, to make a thickish sauce. Stir in the crème fraiche, and season remembering that there was salt in the stock and the bacon. Pour the sauce over the chicken in the pie dish and stir to mix.
4. Roll out the pastry to cover the pie. Decorate with shapes made out of the trimmings, if you have the time, patience, inclination, or small children who insist on helping. Beat an egg with a little milk and brush over the pie. Make a hole in the top and place in a hot oven at 200°C, for 35-40 minutes until golden brown.

BROADWAY

St Eadburgha's and The Crown and Trumpet

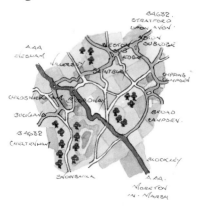

THE Admiral, face burnished a deep mahogany by tropical suns, bestrides the poop deck ready to bellow orders at recalcitrant midshipmen. Then wafting through the French windows the dulcet tones of the doyenne of dozens of Ladies' nights brings the old sea dog to heel and he meekly carries the tray of coffee onto the terrace. For after a life on the billowy wave this scourge of seven seas and several oceans has come to rest amidst the clipped hedges and gravel drives of the Cotswolds.

Today we have ventured to Broadway at the invitation of these dear friends, once habitués of the Publican's sporting inn. Of ancient

Worcestershire stock the Admiral has returned to his roots to pass his remaining days in rest and quietude but finds himself still, on occasion, repelling boarders. However, we are piped aboard with a hearty welcome. Over coffee we venture to suggest lunch in a local hostelry once we have 'done' the church and it is arranged that we shall meet in The Crown and Trumpet. I hesitate to mention that in fact we shall be heading out of the village on the Snowshill road to the old parish church, not the 'new' church next door to the pub.

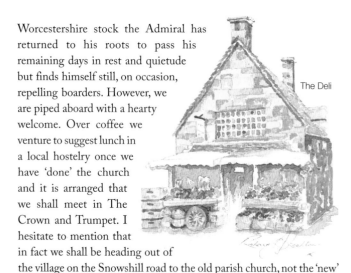

The Deli

Having established a clear ETA, synchronised chronometers and studied the charts we depart, the freshly raked gravel delicately crunching beneath our tyres and the gardener pressing himself into the yew hedge he is neatly clipping.

St Eadburgha's Church

S T EADBURGHA'S church is a beautiful gem of a church. Not an inappropriate description since the legend has it that the eponymous saint chose a bible over gems when offered the both as a child. Like the Godly lady she is, the church gives the impression of distancing herself from the chocolate box village over which she once presided. Tide and time wait for no man and the opening of the route down Fish Hill meant that the centre of the village moved away from its traditional path off the Cotswold scarp leaving the ancient parish church bereft of villagers. In time they would build another church and it is that one that stands sentinel over the turn for the car park in the village today.

However, we have the place to ourselves as we park under the trees against the churchyard wall and walk around to the gate. Considering the number of people who flock to the centre of Broadway this is a real treat. The Old Licensed Victualler is much taken by the little flight of steps to the side of the gate but I talk him down and we progress in a seemly manner along the immaculate path to the door.

Outside, this church is a wonderful confection of honey-coloured stone, absolutely satisfying in its proportions. Although of various dates there is a unity. The central tower rises above grey stone tiles. There are square headed windows, crenellations and pinnacles. Will, I wonder, the interior disappoint? It does not. We lift the latch and step into a gently golden place. From the muted shades of the quarry tiles, through the limed oak of the modern pews to the golden stone of walls and Norman pillars, this church draws us in.

Overall, it is plain and free of clutter. The pews are free-standing and their Victorian predecessors are in use as benches around the walls of the nave. Upon these are the subtly restrained kneelers clearly worked by local people. Under the tower, crossing and progressing into the chancel dark oak is the contrapuntal contrast. Of various ages it forms stalls and choir pews becoming altar rails and Communion table at the east end. Two sad little notices inform us that a wall plaque and a chest have been stolen from the church over the years. Given that this is the case we are doubly delighted that the church is still kept open to all comers.

Topiary in the High St

The OLV is much taken by the Victorian bier in the south transept, it would, he feels add a certain style to proceedings to be wheeled on such a contraption. I express the pious hope that it may be many years 'til such matters are of import to his nearest and dearest but he points to a little plaque set into the wall above which reads "As thou art so was I – as I am so shalt thou bee." Not so much the bier then but "Time's wingéd chariot drawing near." As indeed it is. A premonition causes me to pull out the pocket watch and I note with some concern that time is pushing on and if we are to make our rendezvous at the appointed hour we had better be making tracks.

The Crown and Trumpet

"WOT NO gin?!" The Admiral explodes with a blast as powerful as a thirty two pounder. His monocle drops from a watery eye coming to rest on the front of his lightly creased linen jacket. The barmaid who has prepared the innocuous mixture of tonic water and Angostura Bitters freezes but the memsahib calmly takes the glass and smiles graciously being used to such loud ventings of spleen.

We are in the bar of The Crown and Trumpet, a 17th century mellow stone inn situated on Church Street behind the village green in Broadway. My old chum the Parson and I arrived before the appointed hour, something of a miracle where the clerical chauffeur is concerned, and established a beach-head in the well of the bar where we are partaking of a tot of grog with the Admiral and his ever gracious lady.

We leave the locals reading their papers, chatting over matters parochial and move to the dining area where, under the low-beamed ceiling, spindle-back chairs, tables of every shape and size, spotless copper hunting horns, an upright piano, old enamelled brewery and tobacco signs make a glorious jumble.

The Admiral and I go back a long way and have shared many a run ashore and jolly jape on the river bank or at the Innkeeper's beer-stained oak. Our daughters shared their first grisly green hangover together suffering, from a surfeit of viscous, vermillion vermouth. We reminisce as old codgers do trying to decide what we are going to eat. The menu is simple and sensibly priced, which we like, and consists of good honest pub grub which is why we have come. The memsahib chooses an omelette; light and fluffy she hopes, just like her foxtrot on the dance floor in our youth I recall, and the Admiral, longing for the tang of the sea in land-locked Worcestershire, has the battered haddock.

Thoughts of fish prompt the recollection of one of the Ancient Mariner's bygone birthdays. I considered that it was about time he was introduced to the noble art of casting the fly upon the water. I contacted my piscatorial supplier and we concocted a simple 'get-you-started' kit.

A farmer friend had a pool on his land and so we set forth for some tuition. Tying a fleck of discarded fleece to the end of the cast it wasn't long before he was thrashing the water with great gusto. It was a particularly fine spring day I seem to remember and once the matelot got used to the rhythm of the rod and stopped catching the vegetation on the back cast I decided that, although I understood there to be no fish in the pool, he should get the feel of a proper fly on the end. I tied on a battered and rusty Peter Ross and told him to try and place the fly accurately in a prescribed spot; good practice for when we graduated to the river.

"Your order won't take long", says the amiable Landlord ambling up to our table. The staff, he tells us, are greatly excited because he is taking them on a visit to the brewery that afternoon but it won't put them off their stride. What a friendly and hospitable gesture thinks I; others around the table think we may have been sussed, our cover blown. Surely not, two inconspicuous old coves dressed and acting quite normally wouldn't cause a second glance. It is good, however, to know that we are in a place run by a man who knows how to organise a drinking event in a brewery.

Jolly Jaunts

The Admiral's Quarry

"Who's having the fish?" enquires the waitress, the Admiral nods. "And the Evesham Vale Pie?" Up goes the ecclesiastical fist in case I knobble it since, as ever, I cannot quite recall what I ordered. The omelette is perfect; still risen from the hot pan eased onto the plate and served with a dressed salad. The scrambled egg, salmon and chives is mine, ordered I recall with thoughts of the riverbank in mind. The battered haddock disappears as fast as a frigate through the waves and the old Parson is savouring the chunks of beef glistening in Evesham plum gravy.

The Admiral takes a swig from his glass with a fist that any sprout picker would envy and I am reminded of how quickly that mighty arm adapted to the light tackle. Some cattle had come to watch the casting practice and I was just shooing them away when there was a shout from the pool; to my utter amazement the rod was bent double and the reel was screaming in protest as something as yet unseen careered below the waters.

The reminiscences continue over coffee. The Admiral, totally snagged since that first evening and catch, has an endless supply of fishy tales. His memsahib gives me one of her famous 'looks'. I fear she has never really forgiven me. "You knew there were fish in that pool," she says. It is an accusation I have faced many times over the years, particularly when matters piscatorial dominate the Old Salt's conversation. "If I had," I plead. "Would I have found myself in the water up to my knees chasing round that pool without so much as a net in pursuit of a two-and-a-half-pound Rainbow Trout?"

Jolly Jaunts
in the Summer

THE PARSON'S IDLE THOUGHTS

Come into the Garden

I AM late. Nothing new there the Old Licenced Victualler opines, although this is planned lateness. I have missed the walking tour through the woodland garden; again the OLV is not surprised. However, I have turned up in time to see my Old Chum surrounded by a bevy of beauties strolling in the evening sunlight.

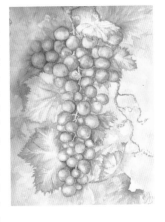

It is the Mothers' Union summer outing and they have chosen to visit the gardens of the local country house, which are tended by our own dear Publican. Having shown them the delights of the wider demesne, by the time I arrive he is progressing towards the culmination of the tour as he shows then around the glasshouses. He knows his audience. First, there is the peach house, then the magnificent vines and a knowing glint appears in his eye as one of the ladies mentions treading the grapes (come the autumn there might well be an invitation to lift the skirts and kick off the kitten heels) before he encourages them to step into the warm, moist atmosphere of the main glasshouse with the irresistible invitation to have a good look at his wonderful trusses.

A great deal of giggling ensues and the leaves of the tropical jungle tremble with delight as his remarkably advanced tomatoes are admired. Slightly damp and disarrayed the ladies emerge and it is time for supper.

There is no denying the wonderful ability of the ladies of the Mothers' Union to turn any occasion into a party and to do so with style. Before we know it a wonderful picnic repast has appeared on the scrubbed boards resting on trestles in the tack room across the stable yard. Bottles are opened and, for the want of glasses, mugs are filled with wine. A knowledgeable discussion ensues as to where the best bargains are to be had this week on good summer wines whilst the array of delicious viands before us circulate. Rare roast beef tucked up in mini-Yorkshire puddings is topped with a horseradish cream, prawns are ensconced on a crunchy half roll with a bed of subtly-flavoured cream cheese (low-fat of course). Sandwiches and mini-quiches of blue cheese, Stilton and sage or caramelised onions and goat's cheese are eagerly consumed as are the dips, nuts and little picky bits that are dotted along the table. To finish off the feast, strawberries perched precariously atop little meringue nests stuck with a blob of golden, thick cream are passed around.

My old chum can barely believe his eyes. He confesses that he thought it would be a cup of tea, a fish paste sandwich and a bun. The profusion of dainties on offer dazzle him and when at the end of all a vote of thanks is given praising the OLV for his great goodness and gardening skills dare I say I see a drop of moisture in the corner of his rheumy eye? He denies all, of course, and quickly sets about putting the place to rights as mugs, plates and the debris of supper are whisked out of sight into serviceable wicker baskets to be dealt with later.

In the half-light of a summer's dusk, farewells are taken on the yard as the swifts dart squealing at their supper. Then the tail lights disappearing into the gloaming silhouette the bandy-legged gait of the OLV as he checks all is locked up before, with thoughts of fumbling in the foliage, he departs to a final glass of cider before bed.

ABBEYDORE & EWYAS HAROLD

St Mary's and The Dog Inn

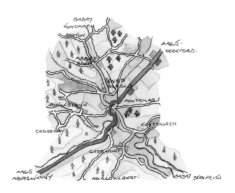

TODAY the gleaming bonnet of the Transport of Delight is passing through countryside that is often described as amongst the best that England has to offer. The shifting border, however, means that this was once Wales. The Golden Valley shimmers in the early summer sun, truly appearing to deserve its appellation. The fresh leaves of the poplars tremble, a golden haze, the vibrant fields of oil seed rape assault the eye, Day-Glo yellow splashed across the valley floor. Yet this valley draws its name, not from some Norman French derivation, but from the Welsh.

I am still explaining this to my companion as we get out of the car at St Mary's, Abbeydore. The Dore, I point out, is not d'or, or gold, but dŵr, water. Now he has problems with water at the best of times. Good for plants he will admit but terrible stuff otherwise. That it is used in torture is no surprise to the Old Licensed Victualler. My attempts to persuade him of the veracity of my point are wasted and he stumps off down the slope towards the church.

St Mary's Church, Abbeydore

S T MARY'S was formerly a Cistercian Abbey. Ruined at the Dissolution it was restored as a parish church in the early years of the 17th century. It is worth noting that of the 50 Cistercian houses in the county prior to the Reformation only two of them are still in use as places of worship today. What makes Abbeydore even more remarkable amongst those monastic buildings rescued for parish use is that it is the east end and transepts that survive rather than the more commonly used naves (at Leominster, for example). At the restoration a tower was inserted and so, as we drop down the gentle

St Mary's Church
Abbeydore

slope, St Mary's presents a far from typical view. It is, however, utterly enchanting. Cistercians chose isolated places to establish their monasteries and although the modern world has crept a little closer there is a wonderful sense of peace about this place.

The Smiling Man

Tantalising remains of the former nave remain attached to the west end of the church, pillars and an arch fade way into the churchyard, the humble folk of the village laid to rest within what was once the preserve of wealthy benefactors. Around to the north it is possible to trace the remains of some of the buildings, a cloister, a sacristy, the door from the dormitory. The guide book tells us that amidst the nettles lie the remains of a remarkable Chapter House, but such glory is past our reckoning now. We pass under the eastern windows and around to the porch.

There is always a wonderful moment of suspense as one grasps the handle of a church door. What wonders will we find inside? St Mary's lives up to expectations. We enter into a box of golden light. Here is space and peace. We are in the former south transept of the abbey looking across the to the north. A golden oak screen of some age and solidity separates this space from the former presbytery, now chancel, and against the west wall a delightful gallery sits on slightly squashed oak columns. The walls retain shadowy images of texts and royal crests whilst a rather well-muscled Father Time stands with his hour glass and a suitably gaunt skeleton of Death leans on his spade.

This is a church in which to linger, to walk slowly around and appreciate. Following the Dissolution scrap sale the internal roof vaulting collapsed into the body of the church. When the Scudamores came to restore and re-roof, this was wheel-barrowed outside and so it wasn't until later restoration that this was gone through and several remarkable roof bosses found. These, along with other fragments of

Entrance to St Mary's

the once-rich stonework decoration of the abbey, can now be seen laid in the ambulatory (processional walkway) that wraps around the east end of the church. Perhaps the most impressive stone though is the plainest. The altar stone is the original high altar 'mensa'. Here stood Thomas Cantilupe, Bishop of Hereford and future saint, at the consecration of the church whilst in nearby Eways Harold the Bishop of St David's fumed claiming that this place was part of his Welsh diocese. Sometimes where the border is, clearly matters a lot. It is towards Ewyas Harold that we point the bonnet to seek refreshment of a more earthly nature.

The Dog Inn, Ewyas Harold

HIS eyes light up as I take the well-polished snuff box out of my waistcoat pocket. Our new-found friend sitting in the bar of the Dog Inn at Ewyas Harold has as fine a set of whiskers and bugger's grips as I've seen for many a year. He helps himself from the proffered box, thanks me courteously, wrinkles his rouge-hued nose and sinks the remainder of his pint of cider. He passes the tankard to the Pint in shirt-sleeves on his left and then to the Half of Bitter perched on a stool adjacent who puts it onto the counter; whereupon it is refilled by the Landlady who brings the brimming vessel back to the Hairy Cider.

"You spoil them," says I.

"Ten pints of cider in a session and you get table service," says the Hairy Cider winking to the departing lady, much to the delight of his two drinking chums.

Together these three make up the tap room think tank. Rosy of hue and thick of ankle with an opinion on everything, their wit has been sharpened by years discussing the topic of the day between themselves and anyone else who cared to join in.

The stone pub lies at the centre of the thriving village, adjacent to the old pack bridge over the Dulas Brook which flows into the Monnow and thence to the Wye. We are told there is a village shop with a post office, two butchers, a school, dentist, doctor's surgery, vets, two garages, fish and chip shop, three places of worship, a library van and three old codgers eyeing us up and wondering what we are doing on their home ground.

There is activity from the Gaffer in the kitchen and the lady of the house appears shortly with our two plates. His substantial steak pudding nestles contentedly amongst a mound of peas and a generous stack of golden chips. I choose the healthy option; political correctness names it the Dog's Pyjamas but the Landlord was thinking perhaps of other canine appendages when christening his burger, bacon, mushrooms, caramelised onions with double cheese and ketchup in a bun; healthier only since it comes with a salad so I nick some ecclesiastical chips.

"They sell snuff here," says the Hairy Cider.

"Yes, I tried some once," says the Half Pint who appears to be the chairman. "Sneezed all day after."

"They also sell something for the weekend in the gents; takes a pound coin," says the Hairy Cider with a knowing wink of watery eye.

"Snow on the top of the hill first thing," says the Full Pint for our benefit.

I grin to my old chum the Parson when, with a juicy forkful of pudding and scrunched up chips, he freezes mid-stroke. I follow his gaze and there is an African Grey Parrot walking through the open door astride a tweed-covered shoulder and dark brown, heavy corduroy trousers.

"Morning Polly," says one of the gang of three. Polly remains

Jolly Jaunts

indifferent while his perch orders a pint of Jarrow bitter, crosses the well-heeled, light tan, market boots and waits for his drink.

The Gaffer, finished in the kitchen, leaves the pots and pans to take up his accustomed position in the gap made by the open flap of the counter and with his hands firmly gripping either side surveys his domain. Here is a Landlord of the old school, a rarity in today's world. He is passionate about his territory and brushes aside any suggestion that he would have anything to do with the ovine-obsessed marauders from over Offa's Dyke. This is his boozer, run his way and he is thus rewarded by a loyal following from his regulars and proven by his numerous pool and darts teams. Pubs always reflect the character of their Landlords. This is a proper Public House.

After coffee we join the Hairy Cider and the Pint on the old pack bridge listening to the gentle voice of the brook, swifts screaming overhead and the jackdaws busily chattering to their offspring around the distant church tower across the meadow. Two hikers loiter, passing the time on this glorious sunny day telling us of their morning's adventures and their planned trip to Abbeydore this afternoon.

We leave our chums, the stout stone hostelry with its welcoming door, open to passing visitors, locals and the sunshine, and point the old Wolseley back up the Golden Valley.

I remind the Parson that I used to throw a pretty mean dart myself in my youth and start thinking about some of the characters with whom I'd shared the chalk. I well remember old Alfie from New Barn who couldn't strike his barn door when sober but with a few pints under his considerable girth was invincible. Like all throwers he had a quick and accurate command of mental arithmetic but also a curious and fascinating terminology for the double left to win the game. Two twos was two Jews; two fours, two whores; two tens, two hens; but his favourite was two ones at the top of the board which for some obscure reason he'd call Annie upstairs. How he'd chortle, roll his eyes and do a little jig. Whoever Annie was we never knew but I fear we lost the odd game just to finish on that sad double so we could all laugh at Alfie's antics.

EZRA BAY IN THE POTTING SHED

Roses

WITH JUNE comes the roses and although we can still hold the odd bud well nigh to Christmas in a mild winter there is always that feeling of joy to behold the first blooms of early summer. There are hundreds of cultivars as any grower's catalogue will tell you; but what of our native wild species, the parents and root stock of the modern rose? They make superb 'structural' specimens and although most only flower once, their branching foliage and hips in the winter are a constant display. They need plenty of space for they show better in grouped plantings in an informal setting; often seen in large gardens amongst the fringe between the formal and the wild.

The most abundant 'species' is the Dog Rose *R.canina* but also the most variable in habit and colour. Some will scramble over low-lying cover where others will climb thirty feet into a host tree showing off its pale pink flowers high up in the crown. The Field Rose *R.arvensis* is always low-growing, its arching stems rarely rising above three or four feet. The flowers are always white with conspicuous golden antlers. Sherard's Downy-Rose *R. sherardii* is most common in the north displaying its subtle, deep-pink flowers against the soft, downy, grey-green leaves. The Sweet Briar *R.rubiginosa* has sticky apple-scented leaves especially pungent after rain; the flowers are a deep-pink almost verging to scarlet. Should you be driving from Aberedw south towards the craft centre you would see a fine example on your right in the hedgerow just before the Edw enters the Wye. This is quite unusual as, not only is it a deep red, this species is seldom seen north of the South Downs and rarely in hedgerows, preferring the calcareous soils of scrub;

one wonders how it arrived there.

Uncle Dick came to look at the Bobby James rambler now showing off its profusion of frothy, creamy-white multi-heads spreading nearly fifty feet along the fence beside the orchard. He was accompanied by a flagon of his infamous 'Old Rosie' cider so we adjourned to the steps outside the potting shed to find the tin mugs and watch the sun go down. He began to tell me about old 'Snowy's' fox. It is strange that after an infusion of the orchard juice how funny events become. How we laughed at the unfortunate man's 'brush' with the four-legged thief.

'Snowy' White was passionate about his chickens: "Why he'd think more of them than the pullet that shared his bed," says Uncle Dick. His one fear, however, was that a marauding fox would one day manage to gain entry to the run. Despite all manner of precautions and fortifications this became an obsession.

Now it so happened that Uncle Dick, on one of his jaunts came, home with an old stuffed fox; it was in a pretty sorry state when he procured it, missing one leg, an ear from which the stuffing emerged and a brush as bald as sick badger. By the time he had journeyed home showing it off in every cider house along the route they were both in a grim way.

Old Snowy had bored everyone with his latest invention to exclude and confuse the invisible fox. One night he was woken from his avian dreams by a racket from the coop. The cockerel was crowing, the hens were flapping, the dogs barking, all hell was let loose. Up jumped Snowy. He grabbed the torch, slipped a couple of cartridges into the twelve bore; and there in the run was his arch enemy. So he gave him both barrels narrowly missing Uncle Dick who was crouching behind the coop clutching a handful of stones he had thrown to wake up the unfortunate birds. I was still chuckling as I went to bed especially about the old boy's night shirt.

Just as I was dozing off, I shot up out of bed suddenly remembering that I had been entrusted to lock up neighbour's hens as they were away overnight. On my short walk up the lane I prayed to St Francis to keep them safe which thankfully he did. But when I opened up in the morning and collected the warm eggs I didn't boil one for breakfast; not just for penance and the aching head but rather fancied it scrambled for tea.

BRETFORTON

St Leonard's and The Fleece Inn

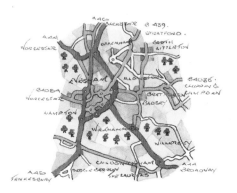

"**H**EAVENS above Stockton! I some times wonder if it is safe to leave you alone for a moment!" Upon reflection I should have known better. Really, whichever way one looks at it I should have known better. On the whole it seemed like a good idea, a kindness even, but clearly it was a mistake. Dear Reader let me put you in the picture.

As the days shorten and the leaves fall I find I have a little more time on my hands. Through July and August there was barely a weekend when there wasn't a wedding or a local show, or in many cases both. Saturday mornings would see a flurry of activity as entries for the cookery/domestic sections were gathered together and taken to a tent to be staged before 10am. Paper plates and doilies to the fore; cakes, scones, pastry items, knitting, crochet, tapestry, preserves; all were bundled into the car and rushed to judgement before I sped off to calm a groom, fight it out with a photographer and welcome a bride. After which, having made sure that all the bridesmaids had been scooped up and taken on to the reception, it was back to the show to see how we had done, gather up the goodies and then off home for a well-earned cup of tea. Of course it didn't always go to plan and things got forgotten so now is the perfect time to catch up. And so it is you find me berating the Old Licensed Victualler.

I had come across a forgotten Maid of Honour; a pretty little specimen and thought to trust to the considerate care of the OLV, ever a charmer in the matter of Maids. Yet here he is embrangled and embarrassed. As I turn and look he has the maid in his clutches and is about to devour her. Flakes of pastry festoon the front of his waistcoat, a smear of jam is to be seen and what with him freshly and neatly turned out by Senior Management and the old Transport of Delight recently cleared of its accumulated detritus by a penurious daughter in search of shoe money I know that this display of pastry pandemonium will not be well received at the higher level.

As we make our way to Bretforton I explain the origins of the Maid of Honour whilst the OLV adds snuff dust to the pastry garlanding his frontage. "Light puff pastry, quince jelly, curd cheese, almonds, lemon zest, lovingly mixed by the ladies in attendance upon one of Henry VIII's wives, so took the King's fancy (as no doubt did the maids themselves) that he decreed the recipe to be named after the Maids of Honour."

Like the BBC I seek to inform, educate and entertain. I am not sure if I achieved any of these ambitions but it whiles away the journey and before we know it we have reached our destination and the OLV is brushing himself down – outside the car I am pleased to note.

Detail from stained glass
window, St Leonard's Church

St Leonard's Church

THE setting of St Leonard's is very pleasing, forming as it does one side of the village square. With pretty cottages, houses and trees this is a very attractive heart to the village. A few steps and a short path take us past a rather grand stone 'shed' and towards the door but we are distracted by a stone arch that appears to have been the tracery for a window from the church at some time but which now forms a gate to a path through clipped trees to what looks like the manor. It is worth taking a little while to read the two metal plates with verses stamped in them on each side of the gate before turning to the church porch.

The first impression upon entering the church is one of shadows and gloaming, the walls have been scraped back and the windows filled with stained glass. As we tour the church we note the kink in the wall where the chancel and nave meet, the well-polished brass work in the choir stalls and the interesting Jacobean carving on the squire's pew in the south transept. It is whilst we are admiring this that the OLV is particularly taken with the window above. Its two central panels depict verses from Psalm 1. I suggest that he likes the idea of being like a tree planted by water that suffers not in the time of drought. Time enough for that after we have looked further I say. The opposite window is very attractive and modern. Paid for by the local societies represented therein it depicts the school, church, British Legion, silver band and a round of 'gras.

It is as we turn from this window that the top of the pillar behind me catches my attention. I am much amused and draw it to the attention of my chum. Depicted is a maid (one assumes of honour since she is carrying a staff topped with a cross) being devoured by an old dragon. Her feet and skirts are yet to be consumed but before he does the dragon's belly has split open – the power of the cross

St Leonard's Church

defeating the evil serpent. I am reassured that the maid of honour so recently dealt with by the OLV sits more comfortably in his stomach. Indeed he tells me that with images of constantly quenched trees and over-stuffed dragons before him he is feeling distinctly peckish so we take our leave of this attractive and very well looked after church and cross the square.

The Fleece Inn

OH HAPPY is the man who has just received news that the cider vaults are full. After a proliferation of Porter's Perfection, a surplus of Slack–ma-girdle and Sheep's Nose, a bounty of Broxwood Foxwhelp, Brown Snout and Cider Lady's Finger from the orchards, the Hog's Heads bulge with their precious pressings in the barn.

Imagine my delight therefore as I stand by the bar in The Fleece Inn surveying a fine list of runners chalked up on the Cider Board. There is Black Rat and Sheppy's Medium Farmhouse. Prior's Tipple takes my eye and I suggest to my old chum The Parson that perhaps he may partake of a pint of the fermented apple rather than the malted barley. He is, however, perusing the ales 'Coming to a pump near you'; Edge Ale from Kinver Brewery ; now that takes me back to early courting days, Kinver Edge on the Clent Hills, a glimpse of stocking and condensation on the inside of the windscreen in the little two-seater.

He rejects the Arty Pharty from Malvern Hills and plumps for the 'What the Fox's Hat' from Church End, Warwickshire. I sense that he has failed to grasp the finer details of the title. I choose the Ark which is made on the premises and is 'six-ish per cent' in strength the barmaid informs me as she gives me a smirk and the local a wink.

"Gave that one up years ago," says another local. "Sends you daft." I smile in return and then I notice a sign above their heads which reads 'The Cul-de-Sac of Lost Ambition'; this is indeed sacred ground we tread upon – we are in the local's corner.

We take our pints and menus and sit at a large, round, polished, dark wood table. The Parson sits in a curved settle large enough for the local darts team with a hinged extension on the top to fend off marauding draughts. I sit in front of the smouldering hearth secure in the knowledge that the recently repainted rings will keep the witches from coming down the chimney. To one side a glowing oak dresser displays a magnificent collection of pewter.

We share a bowl of warming soup, tangy with the flavour of tomatoes and reminisce about the local's corner that was such an important part of my old Hostelry. Unlike the one in The Fleece it was a right of way from front to back of house. It was seldom used as the counter flap was usually kept down. Poorly illuminated, by request, the stone walls were adorned with piscatorial pornography, photographs of successful anglers gleefully grasping silver salmon and rainbow trout; smiling shooting parties arrayed in Barbour jackets, Labradors at foot, beaters flushed with an early morning noggin with terriers and springers on worn baling twine; gentlemen in black ties stood alongside their ladies in cocktail dresses; all memories of bygone reunions, family gatherings and festive parties. Here the more nefarious characters lurked and swilled their pints. Here was to be heard the latest scandal dripping hot as well as hot tips for the 2.40 in Ludlow and the best place to find mushrooms. At times my old chum would be sequestered here with one of the flock. It was usually a two pint problem on such occasions.

Behind the settle, Morris the bright yellow budgie sits in his cage singing away like a canary as the waitress delivers my ploughman's. Now I just love a pork pie and the invitation on the menu to sample a home-made one is enough to turn my head. Warm bread with a slab of sharp crumbly Cheddar alongside a dressed salad makes up the platter. A large pickled onion perched precariously upon a carved out tomato makes me think that someone with a sense of humour is on salads and sandwiches today; to say that the pie was somewhat lost amongst the pickles would be overly picky. The old codger welcomes his steaming faggots on a chive mash, a Fleece Inn favourite

The Fleece Inn

from a local butcher and full of sage flavours with a rich caramel-coloured red wine gravy.

There is a sudden increase of decibels from the local's corner as a chum is welcomed aboard to celebrate his 70th birthday.

"I bet he drinks cider," says I, to my old chum as he tucks his napkin higher in case of a spillage with the gravy.

"Do you remember old Bramley's three score and ten celebration?" I continue. "They got him so drunk that night that they had to carry him as far as his gate and then get his missus down with the barrow. She was that vexed that she left the soiled straw from the pig sty she had been cleaning out and told them to lay him on top of it. He wasn't right for a week or two; couldn't climb the ladder to pick an apple; kept going dizzy if he as much sniffed a rotting one.

"He couldn't find his cap either; he reckoned one of the pigs ate it."

RECIPE

The Parson's Butterettes

YOU WILL notice as you peruse the recipes in this book that most of them are my grandmother's. She was a Scot who always said that she produced good plain fare and plenty of it. She certainly did and she wrote the recipes that she thought worth doing again in her little brown book.

Bought in 1936 and filled with her elegant copperplate script it bears testimony to many hours spent in the kitchen. Interesting recipes would be clipped from the paper, out of magazines and from the backs of packets, tested on the sternest of critics, my grandfather, and, if they passed, pasted or copied into the book. Recipes from friends are also included and always attributed; Betsy's Welsh Cakes, Winnie's Scots Shortbread, Ina's Chocolate Walnuts for instance.

It is noticeable that although the book began life divided into sections – soups, mains, puddings, cakes etc – that, as the years progressed, tea-time treats begin to appear throughout the book as their designated section filled up.

During the winter months when golf was not possible grandma was a dedicated player of bridge and was always on the look-out for tasty temptations to offer her friends. These Butterettes were particularly popular both with bridge players and a tin-raiding grandson and are not something I have come across elsewhere.

The tricky bit is getting the shortbread mixture to spread across the whole of the tin. I see in my copy of the recipe – copied into my book at the first opportunity – that Grandma suggests a palette knife to spread it around.

Butterettes

INGREDIENTS

- 6 oz soft butter
- 3 tbsp castor sugar
- 6 oz plain flour
- 3 eggs separated
- 10 oz light brown sugar
- ½ lb chopped walnuts
- 3 oz desiccated coconut

METHOD

1. Beat butter to a cream, stir in castor sugar and beat well. Sift in the flour and mix to blend.
2. Grease and line a Swiss roll tin with greaseproof paper and, using a palette knife, spread the mixture across the tin. Bake in a hot oven (220^0C) until pale golden-brown. This should take no more than 10 minutes, check after five.
3. Beat the egg yolks and stir in brown sugar, add the walnuts and coconut and mix together.
4. In a separate bowl beat the egg whites until stiff and then fold into the walnut mixture using a metal spoon.
5. Pour the mixture over the shortbread base. Bake in a moderate oven (180^0C) for 30-40 minutes.
6. Remove from oven and cut into fingers – size to suit appetites! I suggest that you do this before it has cooled but if you forget it doesn't really make any difference.

MONMOUTH

Monmouth and Bistro Prego

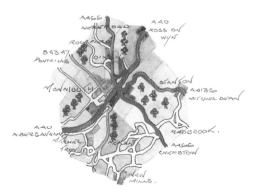

ON A magnificent early summer day the A40 has brought us to Monmouth and appropriately we are taking a mug of coffee in an old coaching inn. I always think that there is something rather romantic about these roads that for centuries have carried traffic across the country. Starting in London and culminating in Fishguard the A40 has brought people into Wales from time immemorial and no doubt in that time many will have ended up here.

We are in Henry's Café, in what was once the Beaufort Arms, a coaching inn where Nelson cuddled Emma and, so we gather, the Rolling Stones enjoyed a pint. Now cheery ladies offer steaming mugs instead of foaming flagons but it doesn't take much imagination to hear a coach clatter through the arch and across the cobbles to come to a jangling halt under the canopy opposite the great bow window where we sit. A wrought iron balcony overlooks the yard; no doubt a prime spot for observing the great drama of the mail coach arriving. The longer I look at the scene the more the sense of having seen it before comes over me. I turn to the Old Licensed Victualler and suggest that thoughts of funeral parlours fill my mind. Muttering about 'Occupational Hazards' and 'Time of Life' the OLV stomps under the arch and into the main square. Later on I learn from a well-informed daughter that some scenes from Dr Who involving an undertaker were filmed there so I feel justified but for now he is pottering towards a man in the square.

It will have been the model of an aircraft in the man's hands that attracted him and as I follow in hot pursuit I speculate if this is a memorial to all those boys who were transfixed by Airfix models. I could never quite get to grips with the combination of glue and little bits of plastic which always seemed to end up stuck to the newspaper that Mother insisted I covered the table with. For others, hours spent inhaling the fumes from those tiny pots of paint and tubes of glue was time well spent. However, this is a tribute to the late Mr Rolls of Rolls Royce fame who was born nearby. High on the front of the elegant stone Shire Hall behind him, Henry V waves his sword to ward off any pigeons that make it through the netting that protects his gilding from unwanted adornment. He was born in the castle here and the square bears the name of Agincourt.

Rolls with his plane

I like to educate as well as inform and entertain and so I attempt a potted history of the Wars of the Roses and the Hundred Years war; not convinced he was listening I gave him a few bars of the Agincourt song as recalled from school days. "Look here," he interrupts me. "A music shop, with real music." All thoughts of trying to broaden the OLV's knowledge are forgotten as I plunge in. It is the copies of Gilbert & Sullivan scores that attract me and the sheet music for choirs that keeps me browsing. The small choir I sing with is planning a summer concert themed to mark the Diamond Jubilee in some way so finding a setting for four parts of a piece by Queen has to be a bonus; as well as music from Singing in the Reign perhaps?

When I emerge with a bundle of music to offer our conductor the OLV is wandering away up the road. I catch up with him outside a couple of bookshops. He never can resist a table of books and he happily thumbs through a selection of titles. Next door is another bookshop with the door open and an inviting aspect and so we bimble in and browse to our heart's content. The wider space of the main street sloping down the hill towards the river is easy on the eye but most of the shops, with a few notable exceptions, are those which will be found on any high street. The much more intimate space of Church Street is a delight of little shops and galleries.

As well as the bookshops there is a chemists with balance scales, pestles, mortars and other paraphernalia of the pharmacist's art displayed in the slightly bowing window. There are boutiques, a fine-looking butcher, a greengrocer and a theatre. This last looks wonderful; a set piece from the 1920s or 30s. A tiny frontage no wider than the surrounding shops declares that The Savoy Theatre is here with red paint and gilded mouldings. Posters present a lively range of forthcoming attractions. We can only assume that it blossoms into a remarkable space behind but a commissionaire is keeping watch and so we move on. Later, as we lunch, I see a stream of schoolchildren pass the window, clutching programmes. It is the serendipitous joy of discovering places like this that makes our wanderings so pleasant. That and lunch, of course, which is now on the agenda. The OLV is giving his full attention to the choice of venue.

Bistro Prego

WHEN it comes to choosing a venue for lunch my old chum The Parson and I have very clear criteria to aid the selection. Information from like-minded souls, gastronomic guides, dodgy feedback from punters with little knowledge, indigestion and bad attitude on the Wide World Inter Web is gathered to give us a shortlist of about three or four probables before we depart. When we arrive in town we give them the once over and then usually end up somewhere else entirely that catches our eye.

So it is that having very nearly popped in and booked a table on our perambulations at a short-listed runner we stand with our noses pressed against the window of 'Bistro Prego' in Church Street. The blonde behind the little bar smiles at me so we enter.

"Quiet today," says I, looking around at the immaculately laid, yet vacant, tables.

"Different from yesterday," she replies. "We were so busy we had to send out for help up front; where would you like to sit?"

Now I have a theory about 'bums on seats' which is people draw people; so thinking we are doing the damsel a favour we sit right smack bang in the window. Although catching a glimpse of our reflection as we peruse the list of runners it is possible that any prospective punter would hesitate before entering at this sight of the 'ones left behind after the Old People's Parish Outing has gone home'.

What caught my eye, apart from the smile, was the proliferation of offal on Prego's menu. With the continually rising price of meat, offal is fast becoming a vital ingredient for chefs to help maintain their margins.

I know the ecclesiastical antenna will home in on the calf's liver and the pig's cheek is too tempting for me to pass up.

With a cold glass of 'Grigio' I bemoan the demise of the old-fashioned pork butcher.

"I well remember," says I to my old chum. "Three brothers who

The old bridge

ran a 'Palace of Porcine Products' in the Black Country; the youngest of whom was not blessed at birth with the best of looks. It was rumoured that people would cross the street as the pram approached rather than look upon the unfortunate child. With his bonnet on he was likened to a weasel peering through a hay bale and was cruelly given the nickname of 'Giblets'.

My bowl of steaming mussels arrives and the old codger winds his tagiatelle around his fork with panache.

"Thankfully," I continue, "his looks, like the ugly duckling's, improved with age; in fact with his curly brown hair and cheeky brown eyes he was popular with the ladies; one could say Oldbury's answer to Errol Flynn, sadly the entrails tag stuck. The business prospered and at about the time of the introduction of the breathalyser they bought a new Bedford van.

The Pastoral finger hesitates at scraping any vestiges of sausage and borlotti bean sauce loitering on his plate. The Parson's main course arrives; cubes of tender liver in a rich, deeply flavoured gravy accompanied by the smoothest of potato purées and as I dig into

Jolly Jaunts

Giblet's pig

my delicious pig's cheek slowly braised in cider my mind wanders back to 'offal deeds'.

"Giblets was allocated the shiny new van with bold lettering on the side and each week he would collect the live pigs from Tenbury market. Once settled on a bed of deep straw in the back of the van they would snore contentedly, unaware of their fate. On this particular day, after consuming many pints in The Oak, young Giblets was diverted by the promise of something warming from a young lady in Bewdley. After a few night caps of his favourite rum 'n' black our hero got back into the van, by now well over the limit as decreed by Barbara Castle. It was only after he had driven some miles merrily whistling 'The Happy Wanderer' that he realized he had company on the bench seat. One of the pigs, obviously bored with his companions, had left his warm bed and climbed over into the passenger side. Now he sat square upright on hams and hocks looking through the windscreen at the passing, darkened Worcestershire countryside and the lamp-lit villages. When the road swung left so did the pig, whilst on a sharp right hander the pig was nearly touching the cheek of the driver; and so the odd couple drove through the night towards the industrial metropolis.

Quite suddenly they found themselves in a queue of traffic with members of the constabulary shining bright torches, breathalyser in hand, checking for miscreants over the new appointed limit.

"Imagine the scenario," I explain to my old chum. "Giblets,

somewhat concerned for his livelihood feels moisture upon his furrowed brow and above his quivering lip. His new friend, however, seems intrigued with all the attention and leans forward to secure a better view of the action his snout touching the glass. With the driver's window wound down they edge towards their fate. Torches are trained upon them. Passing over the driver they linger upon his passenger; looks of considerable bewilderment appear on the faces of the constables as they look at each other and then back to the individual on Giblets' left. As they turn back towards the driver their expressions take on looks of pity for a member of the human race who is so downtrodden that he has to endure the company of such a strange looking companion who can only be transported at night. Suffering enough they think, and Giblets drives through, his companion giving a sideways nonchalant glance at the dark blue helmet."

The rustic red brick and simple pine furniture reminds me somewhat of the old Walnut Tree outside Abergavenny so when we learn that the chef/proprietor has spent some time with the great Franco we are not surprised, this is outstanding Italian cuisine.

After our espressos and a glug of iced water we bid farewell to the cheerful smile who thanks us for our company; well I've heard whispers that we are likened to the Marches version of Laurel and Hardy. I catch a glimpse of our reflection as we depart. Now I always got them mixed up, which one has the bowler hat? Is it Stan or Ollie?

Jolly Jaunts
in the Autumn

THE PARSON'S IDLE THOUGHTS

A New Cassock

I NEED a new cassock. This fact has been evident to the ladies of the parish for some time now and their pleas to do something about it have risen to such a crescendo they cannot be ignored.

My current cassock was the gift of the parish which supported my selection for ordination. Prior to that I had been wearing an old, and rather short purple, choir cassock that had left a considerable amount of natty gent's trousering still on display (this, I might tell you, is the nearest I shall ever get to *the* purple cassock). So an order was placed with a newly-established clerical outfitters and some weeks later, after a telephone call to ascertain that the measurements they had been sent were correct, a splendid garment arrived in the post.

Since then it has been a welcome additional layer in the depths of winter, has seen me through innumerable funerals, school visits, services of Matins and Evening Prayer and all those other occasions when it is necessary to 'put on the motley'. There is a cough sweet stuck in one pocket, past the sticky stage now but so firmly embedded that nothing, save surgery, will see it removed; and various scraps of paper live a half life in the further recesses of the other pocket.

And of course there is the rip. To call it a tear would be to undervalue this rending of fabric. It is the victim of a combination of factors: a pocket opening, several door handles, wide hips and too much haste. As a consequence of all of these the off side seam is, like the Temple curtain, rent from top to bottom. Innumerable attempts at repair have merely served to put off the inevitable but that day is now upon us and a new cassock must be ordered.

It would appear that the decision to do the deed is the easy part. Now choices abound. What fabric? Polyester through to Russell Cord with stops for wool gaberdine and barathea en route. What style? Single-breasted or double-breasted? Double-breasted developed to facilitate mounting a horse with dignity. If single how many buttons? Traditionally the higher one's churchmanship the greater the number of buttons, with 39 being the optimum. This is said to equate to the 39 Articles of Religion agreed 'In the Convocation holden in London in the year 1562, for the the avoiding of Diversities of Opinions, and for the establishing of Consent touching on true Religion' and enumerated in the back of the Prayer Book. The joy of the Anglican church, it seems to me, is that the only people who would choose to remember such things these days are the Anglo-Catholics who then leave a few buttons undone to indicate the number of articles they disagree with.

After buttons there are decisions to be made on the number of pleats at the back, the size and shape of the opening at the neck, through which the clerical collar demurely peeps; whether to have cuffs, a cape, piping (Canons only here – in red), the list is seemingly endless. However, in the end a decision is made.

I'm not entirely sure what it says of me but I settled upon the same style I have had these last 20 years. Double-breasted (I have lost count of the times I have had to kilt my cassock up to wander through damp churchyards, or even pick watercress) with a three centimetre opening at the neck (not sure how big that was until I went and found a ruler to check against the inches), in barathea (having performed a quality and performance check at a recent gathering of clergy in my vestry for a Deanery Evensong). No cuffs, no cape, but I have ordered a cincture, with fall and fringe (never could resist a bit of fringe). This last is an ecclesiastical cummerbund with tails. I was always told it could only be worn by Incumbents and since I have been Incumbering these parishes for nigh on 15 years now I thought I might qualify – and it means I can leave my belt on to hold my trousers up.

BODENHAM & PENCOMBE

St Michael's and All Angels, Bodenham and The Wheelwright Arms, Pencombe

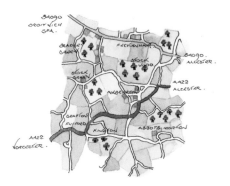

" **A** LITTLE damp behind," declares the Old Licensed Victualler bumbling along at the rear. He has been inspecting the flood defences around St Michael's, Bodenham. "Fundamentally," he continues, "it's a matter of keeping the ditches free from vegetation." His interest in matters diluvian has been awakened by the tide marks on the pillars inside the church and now he is determined to impress us with his knowledge. I say 'us' for today we are accompanied by a scion of the Stockton line, to whit a Son and Heir, and there is an air of the OLV out to prove himself a Man Of Wisdom.

Having pulled up in the little parking area with the sculpture panels we have wended our merry way along the lane to the church. I say 'we' but in fact when we turn around it is just the young pup and I; the OLV is lost in transit so we pause and take note of the ancient raised pavement running along the side of the lane towards the lych gate. When he rejoins us his painterly eye is much taken with the gate and the view beyond towards the church. Before lies an interesting jumble of roofs, windows and high walls with an imposing tower topped with what, at first glance, appears to be a very large pepper pot.

Once in the churchyard we are greeted by a very contented hen taking full advantage of the autumn sunshine and an abundance of damsons lying on the ground. It is fascinating to watch her as she selects a fruit and pecks at it until only the stone is left glistening on the ground. Having recently acquired some chucks the OLV is something of an expert and regales us with tales of their exploits as we trundle up the path through the immaculate churchyard, although a raised eyebrow and a knowing look indicate that the actual work of feeding and cleaning the brood falls to the young chap to my left.

St Michael's and All Angels

A S WE lift the latch and enter the church there is that unmistakeable smell of church. Entirely evocative it is instantly recognisable despite the fact that each place must differ in polishes and perfumes. It is the odour of sanctity, the OLV opines, and we wonder if it is the sign of a good church in the way that good pubs have that wonderfully welcoming scent of wood-smoke and beer, unlike the less good licenced premises that smell of stale cooking fat and mice.

It is immediately clear that St Michael's is beautifully kept which is no small matter for we are struck by the space in this church. It is

generously proportioned; lofty and wide with broad steps leading
through the chancel to the high altar. Facing us are pillars so
remarkably thin that it seems impossible that they would hold the
roof up yet they have been doing so for five hundred years or more.

Two side chapels that give the appearance of transepts were formed
when the roof was raised for those pillars and each has an internal
window-like opening. The chapel to the north is now the choir vestry
and here the opening is filled with a very attractive, back lit, stained
glass window. To the south the opening has an ogee point and is open
to the chapel beyond. It is as we walk down the south aisle that we
notice the tide marks that show the height of the flood waters.

The chancel, a Victorian rebuild the guide leaflet informs, would
have been safe from the encroaching waters since it rises to quite a

height. Bathed in light and with Victorian fittings it is a lovely space and the altar frontal is particularly eye-catching. However, what draws my eye is a small fragment of nothing very much on the window splay to the right of the altar. Here is a fragment of the high altar of Arras Cathedral brought home by a soldier returning from the Great War. Such seemingly insignificant pieces found in churches speak of stories perhaps never told, of hardships and loss, of comradeship and heroism, extraordinary times in which ordinary people played their part.

With such thoughts in mind we leave the church and take a stroll around the churchyard. Finding a gate we pass through and find ourselves almost immediately crossing the Lugg. I am yet to meet the person who, presented with a bridge and river, can resist the temptation to lean on the railings of one to stare into the other. Today is no exception and, as is so often the case when I am in the company of the OLV, we succumb to temptation and pass a very pleasant moment or two lost in contemplation. The conversation turns to matters of flooding, hard to imagine as we gaze at the placid stream below, and so it is that the OLV is to be heard as we return across the churchyard expressing his opinion on the drainage channel over the hedge. We precede him letting him chatter on. It will take more than a passing acquaintance with drainage to persuade the young man beside me that his Father is wise; but then he is used to his little foibles by now and like me knows that the best thing to do at this point in proceedings

Rosa Rugosa Hips

is to get him to a place of refreshment. So we pour him into the Transport of Delight and point our nose in the direction of a watering hole recommended by our Lovely Editor.

The Wheelwright Arms

The Wheelwright Arms, Pencombe

THE sleek lines of the Mercedes Benz parked up outside the Wheelwright Arms in Pencombe announces that the silver-haired, silver-surfing silversmith with dodgy Chinese connections has already arrived for the 'boys' luncheon. The old Wolseley rumbles to a halt beside it and sighs contentedly as my old chum The Parson switches off the engine.

From the outside the building is pristine with freshly-painted woodwork and cream rendering whilst refurbished oak beams around the impressive entrance porch give shelter to some giant wooden

mushrooms. Inside we are welcomed by Mine Host who is busy behind his bar.

"Clearing the lines?" asks the fourth member of our panel; the cherished fruit of my loins and an erstwhile prestigious prize-winning Innkeeper in his own right. He is currently resting but a career as a Merchant Banker (I think that's what he said) in the Metrop beckons. For today he has time to spend with things of great age.

Craig Griffiths (I have picked up his card), our host, certainly knows his beers and while the other three sample ales of differing shades from amber to gamboge. I take the top off a pint of excellent effervescing pippin juice. Whilst they are still 'ummin and arrin' like ill-informed judges sampling home-made wines at the local show I explore the bar. The noticeboard is full of village events with a forthcoming beer festival and sampling, fixtures for the darts team, results for the football side and fading declarations of summer 'stumps' for the cricket club. There is a visitor's book with photographs of glamorous groups of gels smiling and laughing with the anticipation of a good party; beefy men in jeans and bold check shirts holding pints and a poignant picture of a handsome young man whose life ended tragically. In a wooden case there are books for lending out; this place is clearly the centre of the local universe.

With my fellow lunchers clutching their foaming pints we sit at a scrubbed pine table and peruse the menus. The food is traditional pub grub; good, wholesome and sensibly priced. After ordering we take in our surroundings and the notices written on the beams ; 'Fish and chips to take away or eat in on Wednesdays'; 'Cricket Club' over one part and then 'Football Club' over the near alcove. "Perhaps they don't get on," says The Parson. But what takes my eye is a phrase that I have not heard for years. For over our table some wag has inscribed on the oak: 'Who put the pig on the wall to watch the band go by?'

I am just about to impress the company with my limitless bounds of useless information when our host brings forth steaming dishes from the kitchen. Predictably my old chum the Parson has ordered the pie and the Silversmith, forsaking wontons in the wok, has chosen the same, and lovingly lifts the pastry lid as if checking the oil beneath the bonnet of his beloved German limousine. A brace of faggots is placed in front of the Chip-off-the-Old-Block, no doubt remembering days of yore when a bloody pig's pluck awaiting processing by the hand mincer would lie dripping on our kitchen table much to the delight of the dogs sitting underneath. Thick slices of hand-carved boiled ham overlap my platter. Keeping them company is a hefty portion of golden chips and a pair of dark-yolked free-range eggs; other than contented 'oohs' and 'aahs' there is silence as we hasten to tuck in, enjoying the moment.

There is a constant trickle of locals as we feast on the excellent fare; farmers in blue dungarees park their 'Deeres' up outside and with a loving backward glance enter the friendly portals for a quick pint. A lady calls in and disappears into the kitchen for a chat. Others come and go and there is talk of beaters and outside days and lunches for the guns; drivers in white coats deliver chilled goods; all receive a warm welcome. Our polished plates and bereft bowls are collected and I quip that they won't have to bother with the dish washer. As we sip our coffee Craig's wife Natalie, head cook, commis and plongeur, scurries out of the kitchen and heads for the front door; we thank her for a memorable lunch as she hurries to get extra provisions. We are not surprised to hear that they have a busy night ahead.

As we journey home I explain to my Ecclesiastical Chauffeur that in my youth it was widely thought that Gornal in the Black Country was where they 'put the pig on the wall to watch the band go by'.

"Once upon a time I had a deal with a pork butcher in Upper Gornal," reminisced I. "As part of the deal he was to give me a leg of pork. In anticipation we invited friends and their young families for a Sunday lunch feast extravaganza; the leg was that big it took two of us to lift it out of the range."

"And was it good?" asked the Parson.

"No, it was as tough as old boots, I reckon it must have come off a dead donkey; we ended up making bacon sandwiches by the score."

Oh, how we laughed as the Wolseley cruised over Bromyard Downs.

EZRA BAY IN THE POTTING SHED

Autumn tints

I SELDOM get to sit at my table under the west-facing window in the potting shed for gardening is one of those occupations that takes you wherever the current task may be. Even on wet days in the greenhouse the gardener is always on the move.

But this time of the year when there are seeds and plants to order, plantings to plan I do get to clear the table-top of misplaced plant pots, packaging, pliers and anything else usually left in a hurry; and study the latest seed catalogues. It's never long before I look out of the window and wonder at the ever-changing colour of the trees.

For weeks now the autumn tints have been growing stronger as chlorophyll in the leaves has dwindled and the tree begins the process of shut-down, discarding its leaves ready for winter. From rich russet, nut brown through ochre to pale lemon of the Beech and Oak; orange, scarlet to burgundy of the Rowan, Chestnut and Cherry. They often put extra growth on at this time which the forester calls Lammas growth.

Now the leaves are falling as the winds strengthen from

the west. Preparation for this phenomenon has been occurring for some time; where the leaf is attached to the twig the cells have been hardening, sealing off the leaf from the tree, hence the change of colour. When this 'cork' layer is complete the very weight of the leaf is enough to separate it from the branch let alone a strong wind. A scar is left which, upon inspection with a glass, will show marks left by the veins which once passed into the leaf stalk

I noticed Uncle Dick eying up the little wood-burning stove in the corner and the final hint that we should soon need it was the addition of the dog's rug placed strategically in front. I happened to mention it to the young woodman who said that he had some Alder which had been cut some two years and now quite dry. A lot of folk turn up their noses at Alder but so long as it is dry I don't mind it; green, it won't burn as it has a high moisture content but is one of the few woods that will make a reasonable fire even when quite rotten.

Culpeper wrote: "The leaves of the Alder are cooling, drying and binding and laid upon swellings, dissolve them and control the inflammation; gathered with the morning dew upon them and brought into a bed chamber troubled with fleas will gather them thereunto, which being suddenly cast out will rid the chamber of these troublesome bedfellows."

Now a friend had occasion recently to travel to the Cotswolds and came upon a Farmers' Market. Greatly intrigued he mingled amongst the wicker baskets, tweed and stout brogues about their weekly shop. A young 'entrepreneur' was selling game and cooking some of his quarry. He offered a piece to my chum.

"What is it?" he enquired.

"Squirrel," came the reply; at which I suspect the nose was wrinkled in rejection.

He couldn't wait to tell us the story upon his return.

"Yes, but the best bit was they were for sale at eight pounds a brace," he expounded.

Well the young woodman nearly dropped his bait at the story. I heard many gun shots in the wood that afternoon: four pounds, eight, twelve . . .

BURFORD, TENBURY WELLS

St Mary's and The Rose & Crown, Burford, near Tenbury Wells

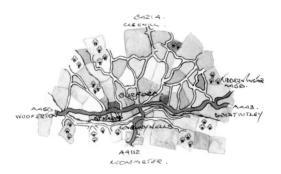

A RECENT foray into the Sunday School reminds me that learning by heart passages, texts or poems has gone somewhat out of fashion and as I stir a bubbling pan of apple and date chutney I feel this to be a pity. As bubbles rise to the surface of the dark-brown, molten mass in the pan, like lazy trout rising to a fly, snatches of half-remembered poems rise to the surface of my mind. Keats is there with his mists and mellow fruitfulness, mossed cottage-trees bending with apples, swelled gourds and hazel shells, plump with sweet kernels. Seamus Heaney has the blackberries juicy with summer's blood but the book open on the kitchen table is not of poetry but rather Grandma's recipe book. Battered and juice-stained it provides the inspiration to preserve summer's bounty. Soon, I trust, the pantry shelves will groan with jars of pickles and chutney, jams and jellies. The aroma of hot vinegar is pungent and haunts the recesses of the Rectory so a change of atmosphere is sought and with a mind full of plans for pickling over-ripe fruit I call upon my chum the Publican.

It is Grandma's recipe book that prompts our next outing for it was from Treasure's of Tenbury that many of the plants that provided the raw materials were bought. A trip to Burford would often entail a visit to the church where tales told in the shadows of giants in the church made me wary of the recumbent figure in front of the altar.

St Mary's Church

TODAY the church is a blaze of light and activity when we arrive. Ladies, secateurs in hand, are arranging flowers for a wedding the next day and the school is expected that afternoon for a service. The life of the country church is rarely dull. Entering by the west door we are struck by how long and relatively narrow, for its length, the church is. There are no side aisles and the attention is drawn through the ornate screen to the golden blaze of the altar beyond.

It is such a pity that the Victorians so assiduously scraped walls of their lime plaster leaving the bare stone to suck in the light, otherwise this church would be a jewel box of colours. Great gilt 'lampoliers' with their oil-filled lamps catch the light in the nave. A good idea, I thought, for the atmospheric Christmas Eve service, a problem to trim the wicks was my companion's considered reply.

The glory of this church is the nave, where generations of Cornewalls and Rushouts have decorated and commemorated from floor to ceiling. The roof, and its various orders of angels, is a 19th century replacement. On the walls are a variety of types of memorial with two depicting Cornewalls in what could either be prayer or conversation. The old Publican pipes up at this point with the learned observation that on at least one occasion when we had a student working in the parish for the summer it was hard to tell whether he was praying or had just popped in for a chat with the Deity with whom he seemed to be on pretty intimate terms. However, the Heart tomb below draws his attention. Here was interred, until it was 'lost' in the early 19th century, the heart of a Cornewall who died on the continent and wished for his heart to be returned to the family church. It was common practice to pickle these to preserve them. It occurs to me that the Publican's liver must be a good way to immortality by now.

Burford has still more to offer. In the middle of the chancel is that chest tomb of which the youthful self was so unsure. Edmund Cornewall, who died in 1508, seems hardly likely to scare anyone today. So fly the phantoms of youth. The armour-clad figure and chest are highly coloured and made of wood except for the lion at his feet which, intriguingly, has an iron tongue. In a recess below the window on the north wall lies a Princess. Eternally awake with angels at her head Princess Elizabeth, daughter of John of Gaunt and wife of Sir John Cornewall died in 1424. Shields of heraldry emblazoned with the royal lion tell all of her status. The story is that she liked to dance and the Publican's eyes glaze over as he recalls waltzing with a busty blonde.

Turning from such recollections I am delighted: there is a giant. My ageing mind was not mingled for, to the left of the altar, stands what looks like a highly decorated shallow cupboard. It is described by the guide book as: 'one of the most remarkable triptychs in England'. Inside are depicted with life-size portraits the ninth Baron Burford, his wife and his son the tenth Baron who at 7' 3" must rate as something of a giant. Certainly the depiction of him in his shroud which lies behind the lower doors is enough to make us both shudder somewhat.

Wandering back through the flowers and with the sound of a keyboard being warmed up we take a stroll around the outside of the church. Here there is a horse chestnut tree which has been supplying conkers for the youth of the parish for some three hundred years. Gargoyles and elaborate lead cisterns add decorative detail to the exterior. All in all St Mary's, Burford has provided a pleasant stroll down memory lane.

The Rose & Crown

IT NEVER ceases to amaze me how often my old chum the Parson and I could have met but didn't before we independently contemplated resting our bones in the sleepy backwater we now inhabit. For while the young Parson was taking his first faltering steps on the ladder of ecclesiastical learning, visiting the parish church in Burford with his grandparents, I was set on a different course not a mile distant in the rowdy public bar of the Rose & Crown. As a teenager I remember I was deposited whilst on holiday from the Alma Mater at nearby Nash Court where, with other like-minded souls, we were to entertain young foreign gentlemen in the delights of the English ways of life; and where better than the bar of a traditional pub, smoking Will's Gold Flake and downing as many pints as was possible before the towel went on at ten and making slurring, suggestive comments to the barmaid who would have terrified us sober.

I do not pretend to remember the interior in detail but apart from the newly-decorated bar and dining room I suspect it is much the same as it was half a century ago. Yet the old 'Rosie' we feel is under significant transformation. 'White' is the colour as the new owners make their mark on the half-timbered landmark having outgrown their very successful 'White's Clockhouse Restaurant' the other side of the River Teme.

So here we sit, the old codger and me, perusing a fine menu of dishes unheard of all those years ago when a packet of Smith's crisps, salted nuts or maybe a pickled egg served in a swilled out ash tray would have been the only food available.

While he chooses an excellent pint of Hobson's bitter I partake of a Robinson's cider; a well-known local brew from a well-known local family whose ancient ancestors' final resting place we have just inspected in the graveyard at St Mary's. We enjoy a small dish of mixed olives and feta as we take in the low, oak, beams and highly-polished brass and copper. I choose the onion, thyme and Gruyère tart from the menu while the Parson takes a fancy to the chicken liver pâté from the generous list on the blackboard which, due to my fading memory, I always forget before I sit down so tend to avoid; besides which he

Jolly Jaunts

usually turns it into a memory retention test. I try some of his toad-in-the-hole which is light and crisp, although the sausages are a little indifferent. My Roquefort, sage and risotto rice fritters are excellent with plenty of herbs and seasoning with the gooey, molten cheese in the middle.

Over our cafetières we reminisce, as old codgers do, and he just gets to the bit where, like Paul on the road to Damascus, he saw the light when it suddenly goes dark; I panic, wondering whether it is a sign from above and my liver has finally given up the ghost or we need fifty pence for the electricity meter when we realize it is a large pantechnicon taking the light from the window as it reverses into the nearby factory.

There are many so-called 'gastro pubs' which serve fine dishes to a high standard as this one does; we hope that as 'Whites' continue their refurbishment they are able to maintain that fine balance of retaining the character and local ambience of the traditional English pub which today is a rarity.

As we trundle home in the old Wolseley I try to recall that week in Nash Court all those years ago and seem to remember that on the last night there was a 'revue' in which, being the class clown, I took a leading part and then a dance where I waltzed with a rather dishy blonde from farming stock over Bromyard Downs way; not the welly boot mucking out type, a little more refined and studying at Cheltenham. We all ended up in the Rose & Crown and much to my chagrin she seemed more responsive to the advances of a young French aristocrat than joining in the boisterous rugby songs I was so good at.

I look at my old chum as he hums some refrain whilst driving and it crosses my mind to ask him if they sang lewd songs at theological college but I think better of it and doze, thinking hopefully of a buttered pikelet in front of the Rectory fire.

RECIPE

The Parson's Christmas Mincemeat

I N THE madhouse that is life at the Rectory there are few absolutes but amongst those few is the understanding that the last weekend of the autumn half-term holiday is given over to the making of the Christmas cake, pudding and mincemeat.

I might well stand up on the Sunday Next Before Advent and preach about the Christmas baking for Stir Up Sunday but by then the cake, having consumed a goodly part of a bottle of brandy, is sitting in a darkened corner of the pantry protesting that nobody loves it and it is misunderstood.

Everybody has a favourite recipe for cakes and puddings handed down through generations or gleaned from the latest celeb cook's Christmas 'made easy' programme but I rarely encounter home-made mincemeat. To my taste it is so much superior to shop-bought (even the 'luxury' brands titivated with several glugs of the good stuff) and so easy to make.

This is another of my grandmother's recipes. For the last few years of her life she lived just around the corner from us and we would form a little procession on the Saturday morning of the baking weekend to go round to hers to make the mincemeat. It means a great deal to me that my children learnt this in the same way, around the same table, that I did and they are the most protective of the tradition. Everything in the same way and order. I used to think that we used a forkful or two of brandy more than Grandma but in recent years I have come to the conclusion that along with the cake this received a tot or two as it matured in her pantry.

Christmas mincemeat

INGREDIENTS

- ½ lb apples
- ½ lb suet
- ¼ lb mixed peel
- ½ lb currants
- ½ lb raisins
- ½ lb sultanas
- ¼ lb glacé cherries
- 1 tbsp Demerara sugar
- 4 oz flaked almonds
- 1 tsp mixed spice
- The rind and juice of 1 lemon and 1 orange
- Brandy

METHOD

1. Peel and core the apples. Mince them with the currants, cherries and almonds and then mix together with all the other ingredients moistening as necessary with brandy. If you do not have a mincer then you can blitz them in the food processor. Of course a wooden spoon is provided for the purposes of mixing but there are those who claim that nothing does it better than a pair of hands – or two if the bowl is big enough and the hands small enough.
2. Leave overnight and then pot up into jars or airtight containers and leave in a cool, dark place to mature. Add more 'moisture' as required before the mince pie season commences.

We always make at least double this quantity to keep the mince pies coming over the festive season. If you have any left-over then try mixing with cooked apples in a crumble. Don't worry if you don't get it done in time to mature it is still wonderful just made.

MALVERN

Malvern Priory & The Nag's Head

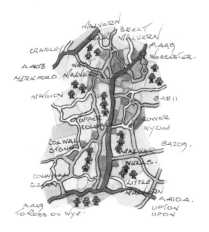

"IT'S ALL a matter of being prepared," I state, airily waving a batter-laden spoon around to emphasise my point. My old chum wipes a splatter from his cheek and replies with a mouth full of finger that he had been a Boy Scout in his time. A vision of the silver-haired codger in khaki shorts, knees exposed, springs readily to mind, all too readily, and then I realise that this is still his usual summer garb when not spruced up by Senior Management for an outing. Actually, now I think about it, given that

Jolly Jaunts

his pockets still bulge with string, penknife and unidentified objects that have been gathered in his travels, either he has progressed little from the Boy Scout or else he is regressing.

Neither, he claims, rather he has drunk deep from the spring of eternal youth. More likely to have been a pint of cider than water, I retort, continuing to fold brandy-soaked fruits into my cake batter. The season of preparedness is upon us and with puddings and mincemeat already sitting in the pantry it is time for the cake.

The reason for the Old Licensed Victualler's truculence is the suggestion that, as part of getting ready for the rigours of the Festive Season, we take some thought for his liver and see if Taking the Waters doesn't gee him up a bit. He has a low opinion of water taken internally but I suggest that Malvern might be just the place. I seem to recall that the water there has been passed by HM The Queen and she is looking wonderful on it, God bless her.

As we approach Malvern it is clear that this was a popular spot with wealthy Victorians with a penchant for parapets, crenellations and oriel windows. Build it big and build it pointy seems to have been the architects' briefs and there must have been a lot of satisfied customers. Built along the ridge, as these houses are, the view from the road is somewhat limited, and the way a little narrow at times. I distinctly hear the OLV draw several sharp breaths as I negotiate the oncoming traffic and parked cars.

Once parked by the theatres we sally forth into the town. It is quickly evident that the residents of this pretty town must be fit since getting anywhere involves going uphill. It gives us plenty of opportunities to pause and take note of the details of the buildings; the intricate brick detailing in the Exchange, the pillared portico giving grandeur to an otherwise ordinary small, yellow, brick box, a surprising Art Deco frontage and, soaring above all, the tower of the Priory richly ornamented with pinnacles and points.

We are tempted. There are two things on the Agenda of Being Prepared; water and shopping. I leave it to your imagination just how hard it was to persuade the OLV into being side-tracked. Before we know it we have left the hustle and bustle of the street behind and are appreciating the calm of the sacred precincts, admiring the noble cedar and the gas lamps. A gentle stroll brings us to the porch where we are warmly greeted.

Malvern Priory

THE Priory clearly has a number of well-trained and attentive stewards for on several occasions as we peregrinate we are pointed in the way of interesting, but otherwise overlooked, moments; but this is for the future. The first thing that strikes us as we step into the church is the east end. Around us are solid Norman pillars, round and squat but in the distance all is soaring, delicate and light with the east window crowning all. We are drawn towards it as no doubt was intended. Build it high and build it pointy giving a little taste of heaven.

We sit to take in the details in the window; the blue donkey is a particular joy. Once again we are guided by a greeter to lift the seats and look under them to appreciate the wonderful carvings depicting, amongst other things, the months of the year. Behind is the St Anne chapel with yet more wonderful medieval stained glass panels, depicting scenes from the Old Testament, here too the coffin lid of an early Prior with a passion for star gazing. As we pass behind the high altar the wall is lined with a remarkable collection of late 15th century tiles. There are an amazing range of designs many with inscriptions, others with heraldry, all in shades of red and yellow.

In contrast to the medieval windows those in the north choir aisle are startlingly modern, installed to mark the Millennium. We are discussing these as we walk up the aisle but once again we are side-tracked. This time it is by books at the little shop on the way out. There are a wide range of titles here and a couple prove irresistible and so are purchased to be given as Christmas presents.

The Nag's Head

"IF YOU are going to Malvern you must try the Nag's Head," says the man with local knowledge. Now I am never sure exactly where Malvern is. That is, I know where it is on the map but there is Little Malvern, Great Malvern, Malvern Wells, Malvern Link, West Malvern and Malvern Common. I am in safe hands. My old chum, the Parson, is like a bloodhound, albeit with a nose rather rosé of hue, and so it is we rest up the old Wolseley, somewhat tired from another hill climb, and ascend the steps at the side of the Nag's Head. It appears from the front as a low, white, wooden-clad building but resolves into a pub of some antiquity as we pass through a large outdoor seating area and past a faded red phone box garnished with hanging baskets.

The friendly staff welcome us in and I am soon getting acquainted

Painting outside The Nag's Head

with a pint of the pippin juice from a local orchard. The old codger is confronted by so many ales that he is even more confused than usual; so they start giving him 'tasters' which makes the situation worse as he can't remember which is which. I suggest he tries the Friar Tuck and receive a withering look. "That was the one before last," says the patient barman. "He's on the Shropshire Lad now." In full knowledge that this may take some time (it took him six weeks to choose a new cassock) I go off and explore.

There is a sign near the entrance which reads: "In light of this increasingly litigious society we wish to point out that this has now been a Public House since at least 1849 and may contain low ceilings, uneven floors and steps, hot fires etc BEWARE OF EVERYTHING." I must have laughed out loud for the house dog comes to see what's going on and as I bend to give it a pat I just know it will be a happy lunchtime for we have a dog-loving landlord with a sense of humour.

I return to the bar to find the old codger sitting at a table perusing the menu and slurping his pint. "Which one did you choose?" I ask. His brow furrows and a certain vagueness comes over his visage similar to that seen at the village quiz recently when the question concerned pop music. I change the subject quickly back to the menu as too much mental activity clouds the ecclesiastical thought processes. The cheerful barmaid comes and takes our order taking the opportunity as she does so to bid farewell to one of her locals hoping to see him on the morrow.

One of the barmen has obviously been away tramping a mountain range in some far-off land, for charity. He comes in for some flack from the regulars, and growling and barking from a terrier who, it would appear, was happier in the bar without him. The house dog appears again to see what's going on; only to be told to scoot as our food is delivered.

The Parson's face lights up. Accompanying his golden, battered fish and light, crispy chips are two thick slices of white bread generously spread with sun-coloured butter. He is indeed a contented constructor as, like a boy with a Meccano set, he starts to assemble a chip butty, something I gather that is strictly forbidden at the Rectory dining table. I have an exceedingly large platter of antipasti; rows of glistening slices of saucisson sec, spicy chorizo and air-dried ham are adorned with piles of small, pitted, black and green olives. A generous salad and couple of slices of hot, buttered ciabatta complete the dish.

More punters come through the door, most seem to know the score and sample the latest ale on offer; the dog returns yet again to be sent out; the barman receives more flack

Phone box, Nag's Head

about his blistered feet, how nice a place it was without him and where was the postcard.

The place is like a charming rabbit warren. As we watch, drinkers and diners gather at the bar before disappearing into the further recesses. These are all individually decorated, some with big, leather armchairs some with wooden pews; some up the stairs and some down, some with carpet others with flagstones or bare boards.

"You're very busy today," says one of the tasters. "You should have been here last night," says the barmaid. "Standing room only." I had already noticed the leather hanging straps strategically nailed to the beams and gathered what they were for. I well remember strap hanging in my distant youth in various Cornish hostelries I frequented then: hanging on with one hand and with the other protectively clasping both a pint and a blonde in case it got spilt or she got swept away into the clutches of some lecherous Cornish Crabber.

The dog accompanied the coffee and put his nose on my knee. Presumably, as the throng had thinned and we were no longer eating, this was tolerated by management. I was delighted by the attention and was reminded of a Gordon setter I once had who would position herself at tabletop height in the bar hoping that her soft brown eyes and sad look of starvation would persuade some benign diner to pass a tender morsel in her direction. No matter how many times you asked the punters not to feed her they frequently succumbed to the beautiful beggar. Alerted one day by the plaintive cry of a child I went to investigate only to find an angry parent pointing to an empty plate, clearly freshly tongue-licked. Beside the angry parent and wailing child sat the setter, a look of surprised innocence on her face, her whiskers dripping with cream and crumbs from the Bakewell tart.

Jolly Jaunts
in the Winter

THE PUBLICAN'S IDLE THOUGHTS

Postcard from the Past

THE Rhydspence Inn straddles the border between England and Wales, the first or last drinking hole in either country depending on one's direction of travel and need. Nowadays the main road passes a little to the side of the Inn and in consequence, although it still looks like a welcoming sort of a place, its wonderful black and white frontage is hidden from all but the seeker after refreshment.

For most of its history the road passed right in front of the open door under the overhanging porch and the temptation to step across the threshold to the cool, welcoming depths beyond would have been hard to resist on a warm summer's day. In winter the large chimneys hold the promise of good fires. So whether to escape the dust of summer road or the muck of winter's track travellers always found something to meet their needs within.

Just recently

there was a possibility that this oasis would close. Not surprising perhaps given the number of public houses that close every day and the speed at which travellers seem to motor by, coupled with all the other challenges facing the licensed trade these days but a great sadness nonetheless. However, as the Wolseley puttered by with style, if not speed, the other day I was delighted to note that a fresh air of purpose seemed to be evident. It would appear that the Rhydspence has been reprieved. As I rejoiced that such an ancient watering-hole would still be open I recalled my long links with place and the remarkable incident of the postcard from the past.

Towards the end of the War and through the late-forties my parents would take short breaks at this renowned Inn, escaping the ravages of air raids vented upon the industrial West Midlands as father's leave from active service allowed.

The Parrys ran the establishment at that time and one of my earliest memories is of Tom trying to catch the empty beer bottles as they bobbed down the brook as it often was in flood. There was a retired Collie called Sam who would spend his days lying in the middle of the road oblivious to kind pat or odd vehicle that passed hooting around him and the entreaty from owner to 'get bye'.

Some 40 years later a dear friend came by a postcard that a colleague of her's had purchased whilst on holiday in the Lake District. The well-thumbed, fading sepia illustration was of the Rhydspence Inn with the staircase still apparent on the outside.

Imagine my amazement when turning it over I immediately recognised my father's distinctive writing with my brother's name boldly displayed on the right-hand side along with the address of the prep school where he was a boarder. He trusted, rather formally as was the style in those days, that his elder son kept well, was working hard at his studies (he would have been all of ten years old) and that his new Parker fountain pen was functioning properly and only to use Quink blue ink. He wrote that Sam the faithful collie was still lying undisturbed in the road outside and that it had stopped raining, the river was clearing so there was hope for an attempt at the trout at the evening rise.

LEOMINSTER

The Grape Vaults and The Merchant House

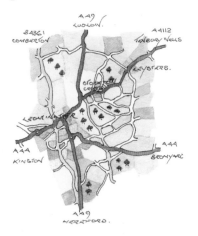

GENTLE reader pause if you will for a moment. Gentlemen you might like to doff your caps, ladies have ready the delicate square of lace-trimmed linen with which to dab at an eye. For as the shooting season slips into the fishing the Old Licensed Victualler has decided it is time he cleared the bothy of his rods, reels and guns.

From his long-distant boyhood these have been the companions of his leisure. He has spent many a happy hour flat on his belly, scratched by the ling and eaten alive by the midges whilst stalking a stag, or up to his midriff in a fast-flowing, freezing cold river whilst delicately dropping his fly in the path of a salmon, or swaddled in tweed, dog at his heel, squinting against the prevailing wind ready for the beaters to put up the first birds. Great days, great tales and great lunches. Here are the leather-cased, brass-bound stalking glass, the split canes and Hardy reels, the boxes of flies, dry lines and wet lines, the guns, the cartridge bags and assorted paraphernalia of the country sportsman. Yet they are dusty, cases bear traces of mildew and canvas bags smell musty. For any number of reasons it is some time since he last cast a fly or sighted along his gun and so here we stand in Brightwells as Toby reviews the troops marshalled for auction. We leave him to his task. He will be in touch and discussions will ensue regarding reserves. The deed is done and my old chum is a little glum.

It is, however, a sparkling day and the tower of Leominster Priory stands sunlit in a pale blue sky, white frost rimes the leaves and the grass crunches underfoot as we pass from the churchyard into the park. It is hard to be morose on such a day and a cup of coffee in the excellent Pavilion Café certainly warms the cockles and lifts the spirits. We sit in

Towards the market

the warmth of the sun pouring through the windows and watch dogs cavort across the grass, panting great clouts of steamy breath. "Life ain't so bad," I hazard. "And at least certain pheasants and salmon are going to have more of it now." The OLV laughs: "Come on lets go and see what Leominster has to offer."

I go on ahead; he has his stick, hat and gloves to manage. I turn at the bottom of the pavilion steps just as the OLV begins his descent; stick under his arm, pulling on his gloves. "I seem to remember a good little home brew shop. Do you think it is still going? There is also a very good garden place that seems to go back for ever. Come on."

We enter the town square by The Merchant's House. The place is bustling with activity as the good folk of Leominster go about their business. We wander clockwise around the square past the currently closed pub once named by the youngest of my brood as the "Three Horses Hoes" and down School Lane. Black and white gables guard the entrance to the lane, looming over us. Here are a delightful range of shops. We pause for a long time by the window of The Mousetrap, drooling over the range of cheeses on offer and are delighted to see a proper cobbler further down the lane. This is clearly also the hairdressers' quarter since there is quite a concentration of them in the lane.

Actually I notice that this seems to be something of a feature of Leominster. In Draper's Lane there is a remarkable collection of charity shops. It is a real pleasure to saunter down these lanes, enjoying the range of shops each with interesting windows. Even though we are not great shoppers it is good to come across a place where each shop takes trouble over its window and they are not just full of SALE signs and mass-marketed promotions. The OLV is even more pleased when he is able to buy new batteries for his bedside radio; he does like to wake up with John Humphries of a morning. He is particularly taken with the very fetching manicure of the gentleman serving him.

As we come to a little jeweller's shop I recall that it was once a china shop patronised by my great aunt. Even now my stomach churns a little when I recall our outings to buy gifts for friends and family, not least because she was one of the most erratic drivers with whom I have ever travelled. She would hurtle along the byways in her turquoise mini with scant regard for other road-users, but also because the shop was small and very well stocked ensured that every movement engendered a sense of impending doom.

We proceed down Broad Street admiring its generous proportions, its range of antique shops and the details above shop windows but we fail to find the home brew shop which we fear has gone the way of all flesh. However, the garden shop is there and we enjoy a potter amongst the shelves. Nevertheless the OLV's melancholia is once more upon him. "Everything," he mutters, "changes." I recognise the mood. Every so often he hears 'Time's wingéd chariot hurrying near'. There is only one solution: pub, warm fire, cool cider. Thankfully they are at hand and gratefully we pass through the portal, complete with well-polished knocker, of The Grape Vaults.

The Grape Vaults

THERE is a warm and cheery welcome in the bar of The Grape Vaults as we enter; locals make space under the dried hops for a couple of strangers in their midst, ribbing the landlord that the service is slow. The amiable man pulls our pints and then, as is our habit, we make our way to the glowing coal fire. Bright copper tables and gleaming brass sparkle in the sunlight as does a collection of glistening

Shiny brass door knocker, Grape Vaults

antique glass bottles adorning the shelves. There is a gentle bantering chatter interspersed with the comings and goings through the front door as people enter the warm bar. Shoppers meeting up, workers coming in for a sneaky snifter, a professional man in immaculate tweed, cavalry twills and burnished dragon's blood brogues; all enjoy their lunchtime libation.

I, too, should be drinking in this atmosphere, no piped music or fruit machine, amongst fellow souls who appreciate the finer things of life. Yet truth is I am as maudlin as a man who has lost a fine plump trout because he forgot the hole in the landing net. I swirl my pint of pippin juice and a beam of sunlight catches the surface, dappling it like peaty water in a sunny glide.

"You weren't as crest-fallen as this when you sold your lead soldiers," pipes up my old chum The Parson. I look at him quizzically thinking he may be taunting my sombre mood; but his look reminds me of my

Gordon setter when I hid the bone: confused and concerned.

I swirl the pint some more and I am 12 years old again sitting in a small wooden boat being rowed across the Mill Pool near Belbroughton one summer's evening. I am clutching my new Hardy split-cane fly rod lovingly given by my father. All spring, a piece of cotton wool on the end of the cast, I had been casting into an old saucer on the lawn. Now, as the Road Man who lived in the Mill Cottage rowed me across the tranquil water it was the moment of truth. I took the fly and started to cast across the pool as I had practised endlessly. I retrieved the fly and cast again soon getting into the rhythm. The Road Man, still in his blue bib and braces, rested on the oars, drops of water leaving rings on the water's shimmering surface. He would gently offer advice and row almost silently to another spot. The sun was sinking behind the trees as swallows skimmed low over the pool and a pair of coots called from the reeds on the far side. The wind turned slightly, more swallows came to feed as ripples broke the surface. Suddenly trout were leaping and in my youthful and distant memory the place seemed to be boiling with fish.

"Strike," urged my ghillie. The reel screamed and the line headed off towards the calling coots. "Keep the tip up," and I looked at the top of my precious rod as it nearly bent double. This monster (in my mind's eye) took me all over the pool until with the help of a steady eye and hairy wrist it was safely netted and in the bottom of the boat. I cast again

Twilight on the mill pond

109

with little effect as my gaze would involuntarily return to that magical, shimmering spectacle of my first fish. More years than I care to recall or count later that very rod is being labelled and catalogued for the impending sale. "Let's go and get sustenance," says my old chum cutting into my reverie.

The Merchant House

"LUCKY we booked," says I to the old codger, as we are shown by a cheerful blonde to the last table in The Merchant's House.

"No pippin juice here," I mumble as I peruse the wet list. "We'll have wine; a bottle," I say feeling better already.

With something white and cold in our glasses we recall that we have visited here before for coffee in the company of the delightful gels from the Rectory. But it has changed somewhat, less of a tea room more of a rather dainty restaurant. Nothing delicate about the cooking, however. Bold, I would say as my stuffed, braised lamb's heart on a bed of mashed potato arrives with perfectly steamed vegetables and rosemary-infused gravy.

The Parson was thwarted with his first choice of a proper steak and kidney pudding as it was ubbed off the Specials Board just as we were ordering. He wavers between the mutton stew or braised brisket but settles on the steak and ale pie which comes with good chips and a crisp crust. The blessed bowl is very well received. For afters I couldn't resist a scoop of home-made chocolate ice cream choc full of choccy lumps and he helps mine host out by relieving him of the last sherry trifle.

Under the new regime the front shop has been altered into a coffee lounge and the 'restaurant' is now open in the evening at weekends and their Sunday lunches are a sell out.

Who knows, if Toby comes up trumps, we may bring Senior Management for dinner.

EZRA BAY IN THE POTTING SHED

Yews

"WHY are there Yew trees in the churchyard?" asked the little boy with the freckles and red cheeks. I looked around at the small crowd but the question was squarely in my corner. There was a pause, not for effect as they say in show business but because there are really a myriad answers not all understood by an inquisitive ten-year-old lad.

It was Bonfire Night and we were burning the trimmings off the Yews which we had accumulated a few weeks earlier. We'd had an enjoyable Saturday morning in the autumn sunshine, taking off the lower branches and clearing them to form the bonfire that was giving us some heat and shelter on a wild and stormy November 5th.

Jolly Jaunts

After the interruptions of 'oohs and ahs' as we craned our necks to watch the rockets exploding colourfully in the stormy sky I explained to my young inquisitor that the wood from the tree was at one time much sought after for making longbows, its close-grained texture and elasticity being ideal. So much so that after Agincourt most of the timber was imported from Spain which, some say, due to its size and knot-free lengths was superior.

Although he seemed quite happy with the explanation, the myths and legends of the Yew go back a lot further. I well remember seeing the gnarled and crusted specimen enclosed in a wrought iron cage in the churchyard at Fortingall in the glorious Glen Lyon in Perthshire. That tree is over two thousand years old and looks it. Most of our churchyard Yews are considerably younger. But the existence of trees often pre-dated the churches that were built in their vicinity which leads on to the idea that they marked sacred sites in pagan times and gave shelter to the early Christians. It was looked upon as a sacred tree and a symbol of life, often scattered on graves of loved ones to encourage eternal life.

Yews are unusual in that the sexes are separate so a male tree produces a small yellow, almost catkin-like, flower which pollinates, on the wind, the tiny, green, bud-shaped flower of the female in February. This ripens into the fleshy, red berry so loved by the thrush family, fieldfares especially. The actual seed, although poisonous, is passed harmlessly by the bird and scattered in the droppings. As the tree ages, the trunk begins to become cylindrical, the centre slowly decaying and as any engineer will tell you a cylinder is stronger than a solid circle. If left alone, the natural habit of the lower branches is to grow downward to help to support the ageing tree and eventually these branches, by layering, will put down their own roots thus forming a circular Yew spinney.

As I watched the young lad spinning his sparkler with his friends and looked at the giant trees, their branches swaying with black feathery foliage in the howling wind, it occurred to me that they would hopefully still be supporting the nests of thrushes, wrens and robins in their children's children's lifetimes.

COTHERIDGE AND KNIGHTWICK

St Leonard's Church and The Talbot

A S THE village elders gather in front of the fire and recount tales of winters of long ago – how they had to dig out sheep, the milk lorry or granny; and younger men, fresh from a day on the digger, tell of frozen diesel and show their chilblains, a painful badge of honour – one wonders where are those who reckon we don't have winters like we used to? Where are those who complain that a proper cold spell would kill off the bugs? Tucked up at home no doubt with a nasty cold.

We seem to be in the grip of what might be called a 'proper' winter and the trouble with proper winters is that they tend to get in the way. Normally I would think: "Man proposes but God disposes."

However, the lovely editrix of the Worcestershire county magazine has consented to join us for lunch so the weather forecast is of paramount importance.

The snow falls overnight but a 'phone call assures us that The Editor has had the snow swept from her car and is preparing to travel to our 'date'. I call upon the Publican to confirm that we are 'on' for lunch. With a fruity chuckle he dubs her 'a plucky young thing'. So, armed with snuff, snow goggles and a shovel we climb aboard for a journey into the winter wonderland. Not wishing to waste the moment we decide to visit a church *en route* and after a mucky but reasonable cross-country trip we turn off the A44 onto a smooth white sheet of well-travelled snow in search of Cotheridge Church.

St Leonard's Church

Cotheridge Church

HERE indeed is a tribute to the unstinting efforts of a dedicated congregation. After the roof of the nave collapsed in 1947 they moved into the chancel, putting doors into the Norman chancel arch and glazing into the two openings either side of it, and set about raising the funds to replace the roof and restore the whole. The different shades of red ink on a patient thermometer, still on display in the porch, record the time this took and it wasn't until 1961 that they were finally able to move back into the whole church. Less than 20 years later

they were at it again. It is entirely down to their willingness to accept the task that we are able to stand in the snow-covered churchyard under the remarkable timber-clad tower, the lower storey of which forms the south porch, reading the notice that tells us where a key may be found when the church is locked during the winter months. With these clear instructions the Old Licensed Victualler sets off on his expedition. He tries to add an heroic note with 'I might be some time', as he departs into the snowy vastness. I set off to enjoy the exterior crunching my way clockwise through the churchyard with the hidden kerbs of graves standing in for the perilous crevasses of Scott's polar journey.

After a while I realise that the OLV wasn't joking and I begin to wish that I had packed some pemmican. Eventually, with his cheeks

Ancient yew, St Leonard's churchyard

an even rosier hue than usual, he returns accompanied by a kind-hearted soul whom he has waved down on the road. It would appear that he has located Mrs Popplewell, key-holder of the notice, who very kindly lets us in through the back door and trustingly leaves us to our own devices. We must look respectable today.

We enter into the north chapel, now a vestry and store, notable from the outside for being built entirely of brick at a time when this was a status symbol, and step down into the chancel. It looks rather as though when the roof fell in they moved all the fittings of the whole church into this space and never got round to moving them out. Old box pews fill the space leaving little room in front of the altar rails but it is a delightfully intimate place and would be easier to heat than the wider spaces beyond the doors that fill the chancel arch. There are floor tiles depicting heraldic badges of previous patrons including some rather splendid elephants' heads of the Throckmorton family.

The restored nave is a surprisingly large space, well restored. With such a narrow opening in the chancel arch it is hard to see how the two parts would relate to each during a service but my reveries are interrupted. The Publican has found a stand with a big button which he cannot resist pressing. Suddenly the silent church is flooded with noise as we hear a guided tour and history begin. Interesting but we have already read an excellent guide on a board and so it is a relief when the off button is found.

Time, the great enemy, is against us and we need to be on the move if we are to make or appointment so retracing our steps, carefully closing the door and treading warily across the snow-covered churchyard so as to avoid the mole traps we return to the warmth of the car and gingerly make our way back to the main road and our luncheon.

The Talbot

MY OLD chum, the Parson, is faced with a dilemma. Two doors, one left, one right in the entrance to the Talbot at Knightwick; he hovers in confusion like a hungry hound with two food bowls placed before it. I only hope that when the fearful day comes the Pearly Gates are clearly indicated for he may just get it wrong.

"Just point me to the bar Chuggs" (for like a buoyant and determined tramp steamer he chugs through calm and stormy waters) I cry in shivering desperation. Suddenly the door to our left opens and with a warm smile a vision of loveliness bids us welcome. For once we are speechless; is this part of the service at this traditional old Inn? In reality it is our hostess and Editor who, seeing two confused old codgers tramping through the snow and fearing we may disappear like Captain Oates in a blizzard, decides it best to rescue us before there is a need to alert the search party.

Confusion persists at the beer pump for the in-house 'Teme Valley Brewery' in their infinite marketing wisdom has three brews of ale displayed, This, That and T'other; he scratches the ecclesiastical pate and the eyebrows meet which is always a bad sign. I plunge in ordering a pint of the pippin juice knowing that the patience of the cheerful barman may be severely tested.

The Clift family tree, Talbot Inn at Knightwick

We sit at a round pine table by a window in the bar; the enormous logs crackling in the hearth, our

Jolly Jaunts

charming companion sips something soft for she is in the little two-seater. The cider glows and he is enjoying his pint of This, That or T'other (I don't ask); all is at peace as we peruse the luncheon bar menu, reassuringly with today's date atop the page.

Now, somewhat inadvisably, La Editrix asks some question of an ecclesiastical nature, my heart sinks as I know this may take some time. I look out of the window just as the 'beaters' trailer' appears bearing many brace of pheasants from the morning drives. My mind drifts back to the days when, with much loved Labrador, I would take my position in the beater's line and then help with the picking up of lost or winged birds. Towards the end of the season the guns were instructed to shoot the male birds only as the keeper insisted upon preserving his hen birds for laying. The elderly, and practically blind, Peer of the Realm whose shoot it was would turn out with his trusted 'man' and brace of Purdeys and would fire with unerring skill each time the cry rang out 'Cock over my Lord'. The mimes of some of the younger rustics beating for the first time could only be imagined.

I must have chuckled out loud at the memory as the eyebrows opposite now looked disapproving and directed my attention to the waitress waiting, pencil poised, for our order.

"You must have the Parson's Nose Sausages," suggests I to my chum. La Editrix decides on the Game Cassoulet. What else for a gel prepared to turn out in these conditions?

Gathering that they make their own raised pie I opt for this, which arrives with crispy chips and a healthy dressed salad from their own gardens. The Parson's nose passes over the sausages and points to the hot beef and game pie. All of it arrives well cooked and toothsome.

The menu is seasonal classics, such as the ones we sampled, with a modern slant and everything, from the home-brewed ale, pies, preserves, bread and pastries to the 'chemical free' vegetables and salads, is sourced in-house; only the fish arriving in the back of a van.

A superb lunch we all agree as we say our goodbyes. Crossing the car park I notice rusty, umber tones of game feathers lying upon the snow and determine to end the day with boring the Parson with some more of my shooting stories and, who knows, a glass of good Malt.

RECIPE

Grandma's Seville Orange Marmalade

ONCE a year, as the Christmas decorations make their way once more to the loft, a strange instrument is extracted from the back of the kitchen cupboard. In one of those 'Guess what this is' competitions it would leave a number of people scratching the old bonce in puzzlement. Black, with a gaping maw, wooden handle and screw attachment it clearly has overtones of the kitchen but to ascertain what its precise purpose is one needs to lean close and peer at the impressed letters along the bracket. Magic Marmalade Cutter it states and so indeed it is.

Marmalade is always a welcome addition to toast as well as a variety of other things – a spoonful in Coronation Chicken adds a sharp tang and it turns Bread and Butter pudding into Paddington's Pud at the Rectory. So we make our own. The warm smell of cooking oranges is welcome on dull January days but the task of shredding the peel to a size that makes spreading possible was always a chore. That was until my grandmother presented me with her Mother's solution – the Magic Marmalade Cutter.

We have encountered a small problem in that the screw fitting is too small to fit on the worktop in the kitchen but we have resolved this by judicious use of a card table. A casual visitor at marmalade time could well find the kitchen floor covered in newspaper, a card table covered in plastic in the middle, the cutter attached to table and two children hard at work; one feeding orange skins in one end and pushing them further on with the end of a small rolling pin whilst the other manipulates the handle back and forth at a frantic pace to achieve a delicate shred which falls into the bowl beneath.

The result is well worth the effort.

Grandma's Seville Orange Marmalade
Yield 10 lbs

INGREDIENTS

- 4 lbs Seville oranges
- 1 lemon
- 3½ pints water
- 6 lbs sugar

METHOD

1. Wash the oranges and place in a large pan.
2. Extract the lemon juice and strain it over oranges then add the water.
3. Cover pan closely, bring to the boil and then turn down the heat to a gentle simmer. Cook until oranges are soft, usually about an hour at a gentle simmer but test with a skewer every so often. Don't worry too much – it is hard to overcook them.
4. Remove the lid and allow to cool until you are able to handle the oranges. In fact you can leave it at this point until the next day or freeze and use at a later date. Particularly good if you don't want to make a big batch of marmalade, given that the Seville orange season is so short.
5. When you are ready, cut the oranges in half, scooping out and discarding all the innards and pips.
6. Finely slice the peel and return it to the pan. Add all of the sugar.
7. Heat gently and stir until all the sugar dissolves.
8. Once the sugar has dissolved, bring the mixture to the boil and keep it at a rolling boil until it sets. I test this by putting a teaspoonful on a saucer that has been in the freezer for a while. I leave it for a moment or two and then just push it. If it wrinkles as it moves then it is set. Or you can take the worry out of it and use a sugar thermometer which has the temperature for a set marked on it (105°C).
9. Once a set has been achieved pot into clean, warm jars and cover in the usual way.

HAY-ON-WYE

Christmas shops and The Blue Boar

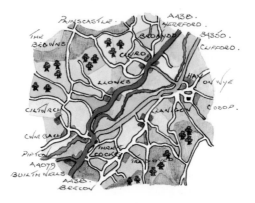

WE STAND disconsolate outside the shop. One good idea he has had this year and just for the moment he is thwarted. Like a sweet-starved schoolboy he presses his nose against the glass taking a last, lingering look before I tug him onwards.

It is a truth universally acknowledged that all things necessary for Christmas present solutions are to be found in Hay-on-Wye. Or at least it is in my household where sometime ago, having endured a Christmas shopping trip with wife and three daughters to some throbbing metropolis, I declared that if it couldn't be found in Hay then it wasn't going to be got or given. To date, I have adhered to this guiding principle. Its simplicity appeals to my companion of many an outing and so you find us at this moment grouped accordingly; to whit myself, basket on arm, the Old Licensed Victualler, a pane of plate glass and a distorted visage.

The bright lights of Hay

SENIOR Management, aware perhaps that her Significant Other would soon be cudgelling his brain for a seasonal gift, mentioned, *en passant*, that she had seen a little something. Armed with such inspiration he sallied forth to gain this favour for his lady only to be frustrated by 'Back in 5 Minutes' chalked on a little board. Never mind we can call back.

It is a Thursday, market day in Hay, and the stalls provide a wonderous profusion of ideas for pressies and a chance to check that

Christmas provender is on order. So we spend a happy hour wandering from the clock tower up to the Butter Market and across the square under the castle's benign watch. Laughing ladies and giggling girls, all well wrapped-up against the cold, proffer their wares; finest cakes, jams and preserves from the WI; glowing citrus fruits, bags of nuts, boxes of chestnuts and dates, bunches of parsley, peppers in traffic light colours, mucky root veg, stacked cabbages, caulis and leeks, packs of home-cured bacon (must remember that for the stuffing), sausages in glistening links; bread, tarts, croissants and pastries; sweet-smelling bath things for the lady who still likes to luxuriate; ribbons, buttons and lace, tea cosies for that second cup. There are spices one could almost imagine brought by eastern travellers from afar and jewel-like fruits, plump and fresh from the sun, glacé or crystallised for cakes, puddings and mince meat. Here too, are the cheeses to fill the corners as the port is supped and the brandy swirled around the glass, or to sharpen the jaded palette on Boxing Day with cold meat and pickles. A collection of those, with preserves from the WI, is certainly on the list.

The sharp wind drives us into Shepherds for a restorative coffee. A warm fug steams up the specs and the smell of fresh-roasted coffee perks as it percs. Wicker baskets clashing we wend our way through yummy mummies and their all-terrain buggies, folk down off the hill with half an eye on the weather, seasoned shoppers sorting parcels and doing a quick inventory of bags, ladies exchanging news of grandchildren and dogs, the solitary with his newly-

Richard Booth's Bookshop

purchased book. We find a corner table with a good view. Steaming coffee has the desired recuperative effect upon my companion and he is soon ready to sally forth onto the breach once more.

There is still more to chose from. I suggest that a seasonal selection of tea-towels, dish cloths and dusters might not be well received, although it is true they would certainly fill a stocking. Some fine china or decorative mugs for the breakfast room dresser perhaps; a bijou bit of bric-a-brac, a bargain from someone's attic; delicate earrings dancing in the breeze; the choice is endless. Bells tinkle above doors and shopkeepers greet us. It is busy but somehow still polite and pleasant. We are coping well with the task in hand but still a few gifts elude us. "Never fear!" quoth I and direct the OLV in the direction of the market place. He is side-tracked for a bit by the display of smoked salmon on the fish stall but 'ere long we stand before that shrine of the last minute shopper: "Get your own back," I whisper. "Buy 'em all socks." It is an irresistible temptation and in the twinkling of an eye the deed is done.

As we proceed up the street there are still more opportunities as windows full of finery and fripperies beckon the boutique shopper. Tokens from here were a great hit one year I recall. At the grocer's the window is full of bread but inside a box of Dearly Beloved's favourite chocolates is secured and as we come out the Christmas window at the butchers opposite is not to be missed.

Rob the recycler

Our lunch destination is in sight but there is one last visit to be paid. The ironmongers/hardware/ cook shop is an Aladdin's cave of wonderment for the perplexed Christmas shopper. We stand in the portal as I mutter the words 'Open Sesame' and the automatic doors part before us, the OLV chunters on about my mixing up pantomimes a little; he is soon silenced. There is not a nook or cranny in this place that is not festooned with something that someone is going to need at some point – and the boys and girls who populate this version of Santa's Grotto know where everything is and are more than happy to help.

As we stagger across the road with our purchases I am not sure that we have added to the total sum of presents for others but there are certainly a few treats that Santa never need know about tucked in the basket and bags.

The Blue Boar

WHAT could be better after a spell in the pressured world of commerce than to retreat behind the stout inn door to soak up the friendly warmth and revive the Inner Man? So here we sit in the bar of the creeper-clad Blue Boar watching the constant flow of cheery souls stopping by for a winter warmer, or something more substantial, served by the delightful and friendly Milly. The coal fire glows as the mellow wintry sun shines on the

polished copper and umber-tinted oak panelling. We place our order and chat about our morning's escapades; the subject, as oft is the case, comes around to food – in particular the challenge of the Christmas Bird; what spiced and herbal delicacies to introduce into which orifice of the festive roast. Thus prompted I tell my old chum the saga of the 'Big Bird'.

In a manner reminiscent of Alison Uttley's classic story of the

Jolly Jaunts

Wandering Hedgehog there appeared in the village one early summer's day a traveller, a Romany who went by the name of Johnny Fox. He found work on a local farm where he lived in a caravan with his dogs and a pet sheep. Very little time elapsed from the moment the first thin blue spiral of smoke rose from the tin chimney till he presented himself, cap in hand, at the inn door. Having secured a promise from him to abide by the rules of the house Johnny became a regular face amongst the throng. If inclement weather kept him off the land he would undertake odd jobs around the inn.

So it was not surprising that just before Christmas he, and his ever-present lurcher, Woofie, joined me to collect the turkey. Since we never knew quite how many family, friends, waifs and strays would be present at the Yuletide Board we always ordered a bird of considerable proportions. Although not far, the farm was somewhat off the beaten track. It was getting dark and the sky threatened snow so I told Johnny that we should not loiter. However, once we had crossed the common and bounced down the track it seemed churlish not to accept the offer of a glass of home-made perry 'just to keep the cold out'. It would be fair to say that this was the first error in what was to become an afternoon littered with errors. Our next was to have a second, just to see how the first was getting on. Much later, and much warmed, we staggered out of that hospitable kitchen to be met by a sharp wind bearing flurries of snow. The farmer led us across the icy yard to a byre where, penned in with a couple of hurdles, stood the largest turkey I have ever seen. "But, but it's still alive," I spluttered.

"And all the fresher for it," said the farmer. "Give us a hand here Johnny." Together they gathered up the indignant bird and in treacherous procession staggered towards the car. Even through the perry-induced fog it was clear that this monarch of the turkey race was not going to fit in the boot so turkey and dog shared the back seat as we started for home.

Whether it was our talk of rapid dispatch or a dislike of car travel in general I know not but the turkey began to attack Woofie who retaliated in kind. Soon the inside of the car was full of fur

Hay from the
Clyro Road

and feathers.

I stopped on the common unable to go any further. It was clear that the bird had to be dealt with immediately. I am no stranger to the sharp twist and pull that painlessly dispatches most fowl, and with a sideline in moonlit expeditions Jonny had a variety of techniques to hand, as it were, but none of them seemed to make any impact upon this monster. We were standing in the swirling snow with just the headlights to lighten our darkness when Johnny had a brainwave. Perhaps the greatest error of the afternoon was to listen to him but at the time and with the last flicker of perry warmth still fuddling the brain it seemed quite reasonable. We would use the lid of the boot as a guillotine.

Somehow we managed to open the boot and while I struggled to hold onto the bird with its neck placed strategically for the lid to do its business Johnny arranged his sparse frame for maximum impact.

Jolly Jaunts

At any moment we might be discovered about our task so speed was of the essence. Bang went the lid, the bird kicked and jerked, the dog went berserk, Johnny slipped on the deepening snow, a cloud of feathers and flakes obscured the view. Speedily pulling ourselves up along the car I gained the front seat and was pulling off as Johnny slammed the door shut, shouting as he did for Woofie to keep it down. Knowing the snow would soon cover our tracks we made for home.

In our inebriated state we made a very late, but triumphant, entry home. With the warm glow of a job well done gradually supplanting the glow of perry we summoned a small crowd to the back of the car to view what must have been the largest turkey carcass in captivity. By the light over the back door of the pub I encouraged the crowd closer the better to see and with a flourish I threw open the boot.

There have been few more sobering moments in my life as the the lamp bathed the darkness of that compartment in its revealing glare displaying not the plump breast and mammoth drumsticks of the Goliath but rather its severed head, sporting a rather startled expression, and a few feathers eddying in the empty chasm.

The Parson is tickled. Indeed if the food had not arrived at that moment I am not at all sure that he wouldn't have done himself an injury but the arrival of a steaming plate diverts him. It is well worth paying attention to. My chum has plumped for the pork steak on a garlicky stew of white beans liberally sprinkled with parsley. Warming and sustaining. My warm salad of pigeon breast with black pudding restores my self-confidence somewhat. This is exactly the food to sustain and we partake with pleasure as indeed we do of Milly's attentive service and warming smile. Pleasantly replete and greatly cheered we are wafted through the door by Milly's best wishes and drift gently back to the gleaming chariot to make our way home.

"Odd's bodkins," exclaims I sometime later; the Parson jumps and the old Wolseley wanders a little off the straight and narrow. "I forgot to go back and get Senior Management's present."